T0275310

TURKISH-ENGLISH
ENGLISH-TURKISH
Dictionary & Phrasebook

DICTIONARY & PHRASEBOOKS

Albanian
Arabic (Eastern)
Australian
Azerbaijani
Basque
Bosnian
Breton
British English
Chechen
Croatian
Esperanto
French
Georgian
German
Greek
Hebrew
Igbo
Ilocano
Irish
Italian
Japanese *romanized*
Lao *romanized*
Lingala
Malagasy
Maltese
Pilipino (Tagalog)
Polish
Romansch
Russian
Shona
Slovak
Somali
Spanish (Latin American)
Swahili
Swedish
Tajik
Thai *romanized*
Ukrainian

TURKISH-ENGLISH
ENGLISH-TURKISH
Dictionary & Phrasebook

CHARLES GATES

HIPPOCRENE BOOKS, INC.
New York

ISBN 0-7818-0904-5

For information, address:
Hippocrene Books, Inc.
171 Madison Avenue
New York, NY 10016

Cataloging-in-Publication data available from the Library of Congress.

Printed in the United States of America.

ACKNOWLEDGMENTS

I would like to thank warmly Funda Başak Baskan for reading large sections of the manuscript, correcting errors, and discussing nuances of Turkish expression; Gülin Özgönül and Tülin Pehlivanli for additional contributions and corrections; Gülen, Marie-Henriette, Nilüfer, Mehmet, Orhan, and Tony, creative spirits on a **mavi yolculuk** between Marmaris and Knidos; Marie-Rose Carre for her wise suggestions on how to present grammar clearly; and Caroline Gates, who made it all possible.

CONTENTS

ABOUT THE
TURKISH LANGUAGE

Turkish is the official language of the Republic of Turkey, and is spoken by minorities in such neighboring countries as Bulgaria, Greece, Cyprus, and Iraq. Traditionally classed in the Uralo-Altaic language family, Turkish is related to many languages spoken in Central Asia from Azerbaijan to Kazakhstan and Mongolia and into western China. Manchu, the language of the last dynasty of imperial China, is also a relative. Remotely but nonetheless connected are Korean in the east, and Finnish and Hungarian in Europe.

The language is first attested in the Middle Ages in the Orhon Inscriptions of Central Asia. As the Turkish people migrated westwards from Central Asia through the Islamic Near East, their language was strongly affected by Persian and Arabic, the languages of established civilizations. Many words were adopted and some grammatical elements too. As a result, Persian and Arabic became as important to Turkish as Latin and Greek have been to English.

With the establishment of the Turkish Republic in 1923, the Turkish language underwent reform, largely for political reasons. The grammar of written Turkish was stripped of literary embellishments in order to conform with the spoken language. Arabic and Persian loan words were purged in favor of "pure Turkish," sometimes the parlance of the everyday language, but often words newly created by the government-supported Turkish Language Society (Türk Dil Kurumu). And finally, the writing system used for Turkish was changed in 1928 from the Arabic script to a modified form of the Latin alphabet. The result of these changes is that today's Turkish differs considerably from that used 100 years ago. In order to read materials published at the end of the Ottoman Empire, a Turkish person would need to undertake special study.

ALPHABET AND PRONUNCIATION

Thanks to the alphabet reform of 1928, Turkish is written phonetically in a modified form of the Latin alphabet: a great boon for the English speaker who seeks to learn Turkish. Each letter is pronounced, with the exception of ğ, a holdover from Ottoman Turkish spelling in the Arabic alphabet, a silent letter that serves to lengthen the preceding vowel. Moreover, each letter has only one pronunciation. The alphabet with a pronunciation guide is given below. Note the letters especially invented for the writing of Turkish sounds: c, ç, ğ, İ (dotted "i," both upper and lower cases), I and ı (dotless "i," both upper and lower cases), and ş; and two letters used in German, but not in English: ö and ü.

All consonants have English equivalents or close equivalents and so present no problems of pronunciation. Vowels, however, do include some different sounds; these will require practice and attention, because differences of meaning are at stake (see the section on "Vowel Harmony" in the Basic Grammar, below).

A a   Pronounced as in "father."
adam (man)

B b   As in English: "boy."
baba (father)

C c   The English "j," as in "judge." NEVER pronounced like English "c," that is, neither like "k" (as in "catch") nor like "s" (as in "fleece").
pencere (window); *cacık* (a cold yogurt and cucumber soup)

Ç ç The English "ch," as in "church." Do not confuse this with French "ç" (which sounds like English "s").
çam (pine tree)

D d As in English: "down."
deniz (sea; also a popular first name for both men and women)

E e As in English: "pet." Never silent; always pronounced.
et (meat); *Edirne* (a city in northwest Turkey near the Bulgarian border)

F f As in English: "fat."
fare (mouse); *Fenerbahçe* (a district of Asian Istanbul and the name of a famous soccer team)

G g The English "hard g" only: "go"; "gasket." NEVER the English "soft g," as in "barge" or "gentle."
gitmek (to go); *gelmek* (to come)

Ğ ğ A silent letter in standard Turkish, it lengthens the vowel sound that precedes it.
mağara (cave); *Tuğba* (a woman's first name)

H h As in English: "have." [Note that Turkish has no guttural "h" sounds, in contrast with, say, German or Arabic.]
hava (air; weather); *haber* (news)

I ı The "dotless i" (no dot used for either the upper case or the lower case) corresponds to the vowel sound in English "put" and "book."
balık (fish); *kırmızı* (red)

İ i The "dotted i" (a dot is added for both the upper case and the lower case) corresponds to the vowel sound in English "it"; in some words, this vowel is pronounced like English "ee."
ipek (silk; also used as a woman's first name); *yirmi* (twenty)

J j Like the "s" sound in English "pleasure" and "leisure"; often transcribed as "zh." NEVER pronounced like the "j" in English "judge"; that

sound is rendered by the Turkish letter **c**.
Jale (a woman's first name)

K k　As in English: "look."
lokanta (restaurant)
[Note that the English "x" is written in Turkish with the combination "ks": *taksi* (taxi).]

L l　As in English: "hello."
geliyorum (I come, am coming)

M m　As in English: "man."
Mersin (a city on the Mediterranean coast)

N n　As in English: "nut."
piyano (piano); *keman* (violin)

O o　Like the "o" sound in English "go," with the difference that the Turkish "o" is a firm, crisp sound, whereas the American English "o" can waver, such that "go" sounds rather like "go-u-a."
boş (empty)

Ö ö　Like the "oo" sound in English "foot" or the "u" sound in English "put." The same as the German "ö" or the French "eu" in "veux." Very close to the Turkish ı (dotless i), but fortunately the distinction between **ö** and ı is not one that causes conflicts of understanding.
söz (word; promise)

P p　As in English: "sleepy."
kumpir (a baked potato sold with a choice of garnishes)

R r　Like American English "r," always sounded: "red"; "party." At the end of a word, after a vowel, the Turkish **r** can have a slight sibillant (s-like) quality; the sound is produced like an "s," but the tongue is placed further back on the palate.
gelir (he will probably come)

S s　As in English: "essence." NEVER pronounced as a "z," as in English "please"; that sound is written with the Turkish letter **z**.
sarmısak (garlic)

Ş ş   The "sh" sound in English: "shush."
şimşek (lightning flash)

T t   As in the firm English "t" sound: "tailor." As in British English, this firm sound is kept between vowels, as in "traitor" (whereas in American English, the central "t" in "traitor" sounds more like a "d").
patates (potato)

U u   The "oo" sound in English "moon." Like all Turkish vowels, always a crisp, unwavering sound.
su (water)

Ü ü   This sound does not occur in English. French speakers will recognize it as the French "u," German speakers as the German "ü." To pronounce this sound, round your lips as for "o"; then, keeping the lips resolutely rounded, say "ee."
üniversite (university). And for good practice of the **u** and **ü** together in one word: *bugün* (today).

V v   A surprising sound: midway between English "v" and "w." If you pronounce this as an English "v," you will be understood, however.
evet (yes); *pervane* (propeller)
Just as English learners of Turkish may have problems pronouncing this sound authentically, so often do Turkish learners of English have difficulty distinguishing between English "v" and "w" (as in the words "view" or "oven"). The Turkish combination of "uva" is used to render the sound "wa" in several words borrowed from French: *tuvalet* (toilet, pronounced "twa-let"); *turnuva* (tournament, pronounced "turn-wa").

Y y   As in English: "yam."
beyaz (white); *ay* (moon; month)

Z z   As in English: "buzz."
zil (doorbell); *pazar* (market, bazaar)

Other marks:

1) The apostrophe (') is sometimes used to separate a word from its ending, in order to avoid possible confusion in the meaning. This has no effect on pronunciation.

2) The circumflex (^) may appear over vowels in certain words, although today this mark is frequently omitted. This mark indicates either a lengthening of the vowel or a palatalization of the vowel: that is, a slight "y" sound is added in front of the vowel, following a **g**, **k**, or **l**. *Kâğıt* (paper) is pronounced "kya-ıt."

Other pronunciation features:

1) Stress: The last syllable of a word normally receives the stress, but there are exceptions. Meaning is not usually affected if one stresses the wrong syllable.

2) A doubled vowel or consonant is given extra sound value, and this feature deserves attention. *Geliyor* (he comes) vs. *eller* (hands). Note the difference in English between "pillow" and "he must pull lightly"; in the second example, an English speaker gives more weight to the "l" sound. Such is the "double l" in Turkish.

ABBREVIATIONS

adj.	adjective
adv.	adverb
conj.	conjunction
interj.	interjection
n.	noun
pl.	plural
postp.	postposition
prep.	preposition
pron.	pronoun
sing.	singular
v.	verb
v. interj.	verbal interjection
v. intr.	verb intransitive
v. tr.	verb transitive

BASIC TURKISH GRAMMAR

Turkish grammar differs greatly from the grammar of English and other Indo-European languages. Do not let this discourage you!

Topics presented:

A) Word Order
B) Vowel Harmony
C) Sound Changes (in both speaking and writing)
D) Persons and Pronouns
E) Gender
F) The Article
G) The Plural
H) Suffixes
    H.1) Place where
    H.2) To where
    H.3) From where
    H.4) Direct Object
    H.5) The Basic Possessive
    H.6) The Compound Possessive
    H.7) Creating a Noun
    H.8) Creating an Adjective
    H.9) Profession
    H.10) Language
    H.11) With
    H.12) Without
I) Adjectives
J) Adverbs
K) Comparison of Adjectives and Adverbs
L) Postpositions

A) Word Order

The Turkish sentence classically begins with the subject and ends with the main verb. In the informal spoken language, the word order can be varied in order to change the emphasis.

B) Vowel Harmony

A distinctive feature of Turkish and of other Uralo-Altaic languages. The eight vowels are divided into two groups, front vowels (e, i, ö, ü) and back vowels (a, ı, o, u). They can also be divided into four pairs, each pair with a front and back vowel: e/a, i/ı, ö/o, ü/u.

The vowels of a word of Turkish origin will normally be entirely front or entirely back. Words of foreign origin, notably Arabic, Persian, French, or English, may have both types of vowels together. The nature of the last vowel of a word, whether front or back, will govern the vowels used in any suffixes that may be attached to the word.

Examples:
(a) Front vowels: *Gelir misiniz?* (Would you please come?): the stem of the verb "to come" is **gel**, with a front vowel, **e**.
(b) Back vowels: *Alır mısınız?* (Would you please take?): the stem of the verb "to take" is **al**, with a back vowel, **a**.

Vowel harmony governs the use of vowels only within a single word (including any suffixes that may be attached). Between two or more words, this principle does not apply.

C) **Sound Changes** (in both speaking and writing)

C.1) In words that end in **ç**, **p**, or **t**: when followed by suffixes beginning with a vowel, these letters change (in speaking and in writing) to **c**, **b**, and **d**, respectively.

Example: *mektup* (letter); *mektubum* (my letter). But: *mektupta* (in, on the letter).

C.2) In words that end in **k** preceded by a consonant, the **k** changes to **g** when a suffix beginning with a vowel is attached.

Example: *renk* (color); *rengi* (the color, direct object).

C.3) In words that end in **k** preceded by a vowel, the **k** changes to **ğ** (and hence is not pronounced) when a suffix beginning with a vowel is attached.

Example: *bıçak* (knife); *bıçağı* (the knife, direct object). But: *bıçaklar* (knives).

C.4) Exceptions: words of one syllable: *ok* (arrow); *oku* (the arrow, direct object).

D) **Persons and Pronouns**

With conjugated verbs, pronouns are normally omitted unless emphasis is desired.

Singular:
ben (I)
sen (you: informal, used for one person whom you know well, and for children)
o (he, she, it)

Plural:

biz (we)

siz (you: formal when referring to one person; both
formal and informal when referring to more than
one person)

onlar (they)

E) Gender

As in English, Turkish nouns and adjectives are not clas-
sified by gender. This feature contrasts, for example,
with the masculine, feminine, and neuter groupings of
German nouns and adjectives.

F) The Article: "a/an" and "the"

The article does not exist in Turkish. The word **bir** (one)
may be used to indicate an indefinite, and a word may be
made definite in meaning when put into the objective case.
Life without the article may seem strange to the English
speaker, but one learns to do without. In contrast, mastering the correct use of "a/an" and "the" represents a con-
siderable challenge for the Turkish learner of English.

G) The Plural

The plural is formed by adding either the suffix **-ler**
(front vowel) or the suffix **-lar** (back vowel) to a noun,
in accordance with the rules of vowel harmony. *Ev*
(house); *evler* (houses). *Araba* (car); *arabalar* (cars).
Adjectives that describe plural nouns do not take the
-ler/-lar suffix, but remain in the singular. *Yeni araba* (a
new car); *yeni arabalar* (new cars).

H) Suffixes

Suffixes are a key element of Turkish; they express a variety of concepts, such as English prepositional phrases (on, at, to, from, with), possessives (of), adjectives, professions, language names. The principal suffixes are listed here.

H.1) **Place where.** By adding the suffix **-de/-da** (front and back vowel versions) to a noun, one expresses the concept of the place where something is. No motion is indicated. *Masa* (table); *masada* (on the table, at the table); *masalarda* (on the tables).

H.2) **To where.** By adding the suffix **-e/-a** (front and back vowel versions) to a noun, one expresses the concept of the place to or toward which something is moving. *Otel* (hotel); *otele* (to the hotel); *otellere* (to the hotels). *İstanbul'a* (to Istanbul; note that an apostrophe is added in order to keep the proper name distinct).

Buffer letter: If the noun ends in a vowel, the letter **y** is inserted between the noun and the **-e/-a** suffix. *Lokanta* (restaurant); *lokantaya* (to a/the restaurant). *Harbiye* (Harbiye is a district of Istanbul; also a suburb of Antakya); *Harbiye'ye* (to Harbiye).

H.3) **From where.** By adding the suffix **-den/-dan** (front and back vowel versions) to a noun, one expresses the concept of the place from which something is coming. *Otogar* (bus station); *otogardan* (from the bus station). *Köy* (village); *köyden* (from the village); *köylerden* (from the villages).

H.4) **Direct Object.** In cases in which in English the object is preceded by "the" or is a proper name, a particular suffix is added. If the object is generalized, when "a" or nothing at all would be used in English, no suffix is needed.

To indicate this definite object, add the suffix **-i/-ü** (front vowel versions) or **-ı/-u** (back vowel versions) to the noun. If the word ends in a vowel, insert the <u>buffer consonant</u> **y** before the suffix. *Kız* (girl); *kızı görüyorum* (I see the girl). *Antakya'yı seviyorum* (I love Antakya).

H.5) **The Basic Possessive**: my, your (sing. informal), his/her(s)/its; our, your (sing. formal, or plural), their. Each possessive adjective exists both as a separate word and as a suffix. The suffix is standard; the separate word is used for emphasis ("This is **my** notebook.") or if used without a noun ("Whose is this?" "This is mine.").

Synopsis:

a) my: **benim**; **-(i/ı/ü/u)m**
b) your (sing. informal): **senin**; **-(i/ı/ü/u)n**
c) his/her(s)/its: **onun**; **-(s)i/ı/ü/u**
d) our: **bizim**; **-(i)miz/-(ı)mız/-(ü)müz/-(u)muz**
e) your (sing. formal, or plural): **sizin**; **-(i)niz/-(ı)nız/ -(ü)nüz/-(u)nuz**
f) their: **onların**; **-leri/-ları**

Explanation and examples:

H.5.a) <u>My</u>:
As a separate word: **benim**.
As a suffix: If a word ends in a vowel, add **-m** only. *Araba* (car); *arabam* (my car). If a word ends in a consonant, add **-im** or **-üm** (front vowel versions, with **-üm** used after words whose last vowel is **ö** or **ü**). *Evim* (my house); *evlerim* (my houses). *Gülüm* (my rose). Or add **-ım** or **-um** (back vowel versions, with **-um** used

after words whose final vowel is **o** or **u**). *Kitap* (book); *kitabım* (my book). [Note that between vowels, the final **p** changes to **b**.] *Kitaplarım* (my books).

H.5.b) Your (sing. informal):

As a separate word: **senin**.
As a suffix: As for "my," if a word ends in a vowel, add **-n** only. *Araban* (your car). If a word ends in a consonant, add **-in/-ün** (front vowel versions) or **-ın/-un** (back vowel versions).

H.5.c) His/her/its:

Gender is not distinguished; one word fits all three: **onun**.
As a suffix: If the word ends in a consonant, add **-i/-ü** (front vowel versions) or **-ı/-u** (back vowel versions). If the word ends in a vowel, add **-si/-sü** (front vowel versions) or **-sı/-su** (back vowel versions). [The **s** serves here as a buffer consonant between the two vowels.] *Arabası* (his/her car).

H.5.d) Our:

As a separate word: **bizim**.
As a suffix: If the word ends in a vowel, add **-miz/-müz** (front vowel versions) or **-mız/-muz** (back vowel versions). If the word ends in a consonant, add **-imiz/-ümüz** (front vowel versions) or **-ımız/-umuz** (back vowel versions). *Arabamız* (our car).

H.5.e) Your (sing. formal, or plural):

As a separate word: **sizin**.
As a suffix: If the word ends in a vowel, add **-niz/-nüz** (front vowel versions) or **-nız/-nuz** (back vowel versions). If the word ends in a consonant, add **-iniz/-ünüz** (front vowel versions) or **-ınız/-unuz** (back vowel versions). *Arabanız* (your car). *Muz* (banana);

muzunuz (your banana); but note: *muzlarınız* (your bananas).

H.5.f) Their:

As a separate word: **onların**.

As a suffix: Add **-leri** (front vowel version) or **-ları** (back vowel version) to a singular noun. *Evleri* (their house); *arabaları* (their car). But note that the same form is used even when the noun is plural: *evleri* (their houses), not "evlerleri." Context will make clear the exact meaning.

H.6) **The Compound Possessive.** Used in the third person only, singular and plural, when both the possessor and the thing possessed are expressed, for example, "Ali's hat" or "the man's shirt." Each noun carries a suffix, and they are different. To learn this pattern, it may be helpful to think of phrases such as "of Ali, his hat," or "of the man, his shirt."

The suffix for the thing possessed has already been learned: **-i/-ü** or **-ı/-u** (preceded by the buffer consonant **s** if the word ends in a vowel), as noted above under H.5.c: "his/her/its." For the plural, the suffix is **-leri/-ları**, as given above under H.5.f: "their."

The suffix for the possessor: If the word ends in a consonant, add **-in/-ün** (front vowel versions) or **-ın/-un** (back vowel versions). *Adam* (man); *adamın* (man's). If the word ends in a vowel, add **-nin/-nün** (front vowel versions) or **-nın/-nun** (back vowel versions). *Kedi* (cat); *kedinin* (cat's). *Gülru* (a woman's name); *Gülru'nun* (Gülru's). [Note: In written Turkish, proper names are usually separated from the suffix with an apostrophe, in order to avoid confusion.]

Examples: *Ali'nin şapkası* (Ali's hat). *Adamın evi* (the man's house). *Adamların evi* (the men's house). *Hanım* (lady); *hanımın kitapları* (the lady's books).

But: If, in a combination of two nouns, the first noun is a modifier rather than a possessor, it does not take a separate suffix. *Ziraat* (agriculture); *banka* (bank); but together: *Ziraat Bankası* (the Agriculture Bank, the largest of the state-owned banks). *Atatürk Havalimanı* (the Atatürk Airport, in Istanbul). *Üniversite* (university); *Ankara Üniversitesi* (Ankara University).

The possessive combined with other suffixes: Form the possessive first, then add one or more suffixes. The consonant **n** is inserted as a buffer letter before Suffix H.1, H.2, H.3, or H.4 is added.

Examples: *Ali'nin evi* (Ali's house); *Ali'nin evinde* (at Ali's house); *Ali'nin evine* (to Ali's house); *Ali'nin evini* (Ali's house, with the definite or direct object suffix); *Ali'nin evlerinden* (from Ali's houses).

H.7) **Creating a Noun.** To form a noun from an adjective, add the suffix **-lik/-lük** (front vowel versions) or **-lık/-luk** (back vowel versions) to the adjective. *Hasta* (sick); *hastalık* (illness).

H.8) **Creating an Adjective.** To make an adjective from a noun, add the suffix **-li/-lü** (front vowel versions) or **-lı/-lu** (back vowel versions). *Süt* (milk); *sütlü* (milky, with milk). *Zarar* (damage, harm); *zararlı* (harmful, damaging).

H.9) **Profession.** To indicate a profession, add to a noun the suffix **-ci/-cü** (front vowel versions) or **-cı/cu** (back vowel versions). *Kapı* (door); *kapıcı* (doorman, concierge). *İş* (work); *işçi* (worker, workman). <u>Note</u>: after the unvocalized ş, the Turkish **c** (vocalized) changes to **ç** (unvocalized).

H.10) **Language.** To form the name of a language, add the suffix **-ce/-ca** to the adjective that describes an ethnic group. *İngiliz* (*adj.* English); *İngilizce* (English language). *Fransız* (*adj.* French); *Fransızca* (French language). *Türk* (*adj.* Turkish); *Türkçe* (Turkish language). <u>Note</u>: The vocalized **c** of the suffix becomes an unvocalized **ç** when added to a word ending in an unvocalized consonant.

H.11) **With.** "Together with" or "by means of" is expressed by the separate word **ile** or by the suffix **-le/-la** (front and back vowel versions). *Otobüs* (bus); *otobüsle* (by bus). *Uçak* (airplane); *uçakla* (by airplane; airmail). *Arkadaş* (friend); *arkadaşla* (with a/the friend).

H.12) **Without.** Add to a noun the suffix **-siz/-süz** (front vowel versions) or **-sız/-suz** (back vowel versions). *Şeker* (sugar); *şekersiz* (without sugar). *Tuz* (salt); *tuzsuz* (without salt).

I) Adjectives

An adjective normally comes before the modified noun. It has one form only; that is, it does not take on the suffixes that the noun may have. *Güzel* (beautiful). *Güzel ev* (a/the beautiful house); *güzel evler* (beautiful houses); *güzel evlerden* (from the beautiful houses).

Some adjectives may also serve as adverbs: *iyi* (good, well); *çok* (many, much, very).

J) Adverbs

Like adjectives, adverbs have one form only. An adverb normally is placed before the verb that it modifies.

For emphasis or for use especially in the written language, some adverbs feature a variant in which the word is doubled: *yavaş* (slowly, gently) or *yavaş yavaş*.

K) Comparison of Adjectives and Adverbs

The comparative form of an adjective or adverb is created by placing the word **daha** (more) or **daha az** (less) in front of the adjective or adverb. The item compared is indicated by **-den/-dan** (for English "than").

Examples: *Bu ev daha büyük.* (This house is bigger.) *Otobüsle gitmek yürümekten daha az yorucu.* (To go with the bus is less tiring than to walk.) *Şu evden bu ev daha büyük.* (This house is bigger than that house.) *Benim evim Mehmet Bey'in evinden daha güzel.* (My house is more beautiful than Mehmet Bey's house.)

The superlative form of an adjective or adverb is created by placing the word **en** (most) in front of the adjective or adverb.

Examples: *en güzel çiçek* (the most beautiful flower). *Türkiye'nin en büyük şehri İstanbul'dur.* (Turkey's biggest city is Istanbul.) *En hızlı koşan çocuk Hilmi'dir.* (Hilmi is the boy who runs the fastest. *lit.* The fastest running boy is Hilmi.)

L) Postpositions

English prepositional phrases can be expressed not only by means of suffixes (see H, above), but also by <u>postpositions</u>, words that follow the noun to which they refer. In certain cases, the noun is left plain. Other postpositions follow nouns to which either the **-e/-a** suffix or the **-den/-dan** suffix must be attached. By practice, one learns which postpositions require which suffix (or none at all). The principal postpositions are given below, in three groups:

L.1) <u>Nouns without a suffix</u> + <u>postposition</u>

L.1.a) **gibi** (like): *buz gibi su* (ice-cold water, *lit.* ice-like water)

L.1.b) **için** (for): *öğrenciler için* (for the students)

L.1.c) **ile** (with, by means of): *uçak ile* (via airmail)
Note: *İle* can also be expressed by the suffix **-le/-la.**

L.1.d) **kadar** (as ... as): *Ayşe, Pınar kadar akıllı bir çocuk.* (Ayşe is as intelligent a child as Pınar.)
Note: A comma sets Ayşe off from Pınar, in order to make absolutely clear that Ayşe and Pınar are not one person, but two different people.

L.2) <u>Nouns with an **-e/-a** suffix</u> + <u>postposition</u>

L.2.a) **doğru** (towards, near): *akşama doğru* (towards the evening)

L.2.b) **göre** (according to): *öğretmene göre* (according to the teacher)

L.2.c) **kadar** (as far as, until): *Ankara'ya kadar gidiyoruz.* (We are going as far as Ankara.)

L.2.d) **karşı** (opposite, across from, against): *İşadamı enflasyona karşı konuştu.* (The businessman spoke against inflation.)

L.3) <u>Nouns with a **-den/-dan** suffix</u> + <u>postposition</u>

L.3.a) **başka** (other than, besides): *Kızım ıspanaktan başka tüm sebzeleri yiyor.* (Other than spinach, my daughter eats all vegetables.)

L.3.b) **beri** (since): *Ocak ayından beri toplantılara katılmıyor.* (Since January he hasn't participated in the meetings.)

L.3.c) **önce** (before): *Konserden önce lokantada akşam yemeği yedik.* (Before the concert, we ate dinner in the restaurant.)

L.3.d) **sonra** (after): *Konserden sonra eve gideceğiz.* (After the concert we shall go home.)

M) Conjunctions and Interjections

With one exception, these words are used as in English. Frequently used <u>conjunctions</u> include: **ve** (and), **veya** (or), and **ama** or **fakat** (but). Frequently used <u>interjections</u> include: **Aferin!** (well done!), **Haydi!** (come on!), **İnşallah** (God willing; I hope that …), and **Maşallah!** (wonderful!).

A distinctive construction that can be used to avoid a conjunction when listing one or more actions that follow one another is the suffix **-ip/-ıp/-üp/-up**. In English, this suffix can be translated as "and." When connecting two or more verbs, this suffix is attached to the stem form of the initial verb or verbs. The final verb is conjugated in the normal way. No additional conjunctions are needed. The initial verb or verbs take on the mood and tense of the final verb.

Example: *Ofise gidip mektubu yazdı.* (He went to the office and wrote the letter.)

N) The Negative

Turkish has three ways to express the negative, "not."

(1) The word **değil** is used with the verb "to be" (see Section Q.10.c, below).
(2) The word **yok** is used specifically when meaning "there is not" or "there are not." It is the negative of **var**, which means "there is" or "there are" (see Section Q.11, below).
(3) The negative particle **-me/-ma** is used with all other verbs (see Section Q.6, below).

All three types of negatives are explained further, with examples, in the section on verbs below.

O) Asking a Question

In Turkish, a question is indicated by using either a "question word" or the "interrogative particle" **mi/mı/mü/mu**. Unlike English, the word order of a sentence does not change when a question is asked. The interrogative particle can be used only once per sentence. It can be placed either after or (in the case of conjugated verbs) within any element in the sentence about which the question is raised. The syllable preceding the particle takes the stress. The particle is <u>never</u> attached as a suffix, but is written with an intervening space. However, it can have its own suffixes (see example below).

Note the similarity between the interrogative particle **mi/mı/mü/mu** and the negative element **-me/-ma**. Because each has its distinctive, defined place in a sentence, confusion is avoided. The negative particle is placed immediately after the verb stem, whereas the interrogative particle is placed after the tense marker. See Section Q.7, Present Tense, Active, for examples of the <u>negative</u>, the <u>question</u>, and the <u>negative question</u>.

Question words include: **kim** (who?), **nasıl** (how?), **ne** (what?), **nerede** (where?), **kaç** (how many?), **niçin** (why?), etc.

Examples using the interrogative particle: *Bu lokanta iyi mi?* (Is this restaurant good?); *Nasılsınız? İyi misiniz?* (How are you? Are you well?); *Hesabı getirir misiniz?* (Would you please bring the bill?).

Değil mi?: This combination of **değil** (not) and the interrogative particle is used to express the English "isn't it?" and its variants, at the end of questions. Unlike English, this two-word phrase never changes. In this, it resembles the French "n'est-ce pas?": *Bu plaj çok güzel, değil mi?* (This beach is very beautiful, isn't it?).

P) Agreeing with a Negative Statement

This feature is best illustrated with an anecdote. I was recently admiring two bonsai trees in a restaurant in

Ankara. Then I realized they were artificial. *Ah, gerçek değiller!* ("Oh, they are not real!"), I exclaimed. *Evet* ("Yes"), the waiter replied.

An English-speaking waiter would have agreed with me by saying, "No." (No, indeed they are not real.) What the Turkish waiter meant by answering "Yes," was: "Yes, I agree with you; the trees are not real." Mastering the correct use of **evet** (yes) in this situation, when our English speaker's instinct urges us to say **hayır** (no), takes much patience and practice.

Q) Verbs

The Turkish verb system has three main characteristics.

<u>First</u>, verbs are, in general, regular. This fact will come as a huge relief to anyone who has struggled to memorize the countless irregular verb forms of French, Spanish, and other Indo-European languages.

<u>Second</u>, mood, tense, and person are indicated by suffixes added (in a systematic manner) to the verb stem. Instead of the English reliance on auxiliary words, the Turkish verb, whatever its mood or tense, is written as one single word. This word might be long, but with experience one learns to recognize more and more quickly the telling elements.

Example (a banner recently observed in Ankara): *İş yerimiz Çankaya Belediyesi tarafından Mavi bayrak'la ödüllendirilmiştir.* (Our workplace <u>has been awarded</u> with a Blue Flag by the Çankaya Municipality.) The verb—**ödüllendirilmiştir**—comes from (1) **ödül** (prize, award); (2) **-lendir-** (which creates a verb from the noun = to award a prize); (3) **-il-** (which turns active into passive = to be awarded a prize); and (4) **-miştir** (a formal version of the past tense ending, third person singular).

Third, the moods and tenses of Turkish sometimes correspond to those of English, but there are numerous differences, too. This presentation offers a selection of frequently used forms.

Note: The rules of vowel harmony (see Section B) continue throughout the verb system, with mood and tense markers having both front and back vowel versions. I give both versions for each new set of verb forms when it would seem particularly helpful, but otherwise will limit myself to only one version, as representative.

Q.1) **Verb Stem and Active Infinitive**: to come

Formula: verb stem + **-mek** (front vowel version)/**-mak** (back vowel version)

Examples: **gel** + **mek** → *gelmek* (to come); **al** + **mak** → *almak* (to take).

Q.2) **Passive Infinitive**: to be given

Formula: verb stem + **-il/-ıl/-ül/-ul** + **-mek/-mak**

Exceptions: If the verb stem ends in a vowel, add **n**; if the verb stem ends in l, add **-in/-ın/-ün/-un**.

Examples: **ver** + **il** + **mek** → *verilmek* (to be given); **iste** + **n** + **mek** → *istenmek* (to be wanted); **bul** + **un** + **mak** → *bulunmak* (to be found).

Q.3) **Causative Infinitive**: to cause to do something; to have (someone) do something

Formula (most common): verb stem + **-dir/-dır/-dür/ -dur** [**-tir**, etc., after unvoiced consonants] + **-mek/-mak**

Another formula (also common): polysyllabic verb stem that ends in a vowel + **t** + **-mek/-mak**

Examples: **silmek** (to wipe); **sil** + **dir** + **mek** (to have someone wipe). *Mehmet'e tahtayı sildirdim.* (I had Mehmet wipe the blackboard.) **beklemek** (to wait); **bekle** + **t** + **mek** (to cause [someone] to wait, to make [s.o.] wait). *Sizi beklettim.* (I made you wait.)

Q.4) **Auxiliary Verbs**

Etmek is the main auxiliary verb. *Etmek*, meaning "to do, to make," is not used by itself, but is joined with a noun, especially one of non-Turkish origin, to create a verb. *Etmek* is conjugated like all other verbs.

Examples: *telefon etmek* (to telephone); *ziyaret etmek* (to visit).

Q.5) **Verbs: Personal Endings.** The tenses presented below end with one of the following two types of personal endings:

Type I: Used with present, "miş" past, future, and "aorist" tenses.

Sing:	1st person:	**-im/-ım/-üm/-um**
	2nd person:	**-sin/-sın/-sün/-sun**
	3rd person:	— (no ending)
Pl:	1st person:	**-iz/-ız/-üz/-uz**
	2nd person:	**-siniz/-sınız/-sünüz/-sunuz**
	3rd person:	**-ler/-lar**

Type II: Used with simple past, pluperfect, imperfect, future past, and "aorist" past tenses.

Sing: 1st person: **-m**
          2nd person: **-n**
          3rd person: — (no ending)
Pl: 1st person: **-k**
          2nd person: **-niz/-nız/-nüz/-nuz**
          3rd person: **-ler/-lar**

Q.6) **The Negative, for verb tenses other than "to be."** This is expressed by placing the element **-me-/-ma-** directly after the verb stem, before the tense marker and the personal endings. The vowel **e** or **a** disappears if the tense marker starts with a vowel. The negative syllable is unaccented; the accent falls on the preceding syllable. Examples are given below, for each tense, with variant forms noted.

Q.7) **Present, Active**: I come; I am coming

Q.7.a) Formula (Positive): verb stem + **-iyor/-ıyor/ -üyor/-uyor** (present marker) + Type I personal endings

Example with front vowels: *gelmek* (to come)
Sing: *geliyorum, geliyorsun, geliyor* (I come; you come; he/she/it comes)
Pl: *geliyoruz, geliyorsunuz, geliyorlar* (we come; you come; they come)

Example with back vowels: *almak* (to take)
Sing: *alıyorum, alıyorsun, alıyor* (I take; you take; he/she/it takes)
Pl: *alıyoruz, alıyorsunuz, alıyorlar* (we take; you take; they take)

Q.7.b) <u>Negative</u>:

Sing: *gelmiyorum, gelmiyorsun, gelmiyor* (I do not come; you do not come; he/she/it does not come)

Pl: *gelmiyoruz, gelmiyorsunuz, gemiyorlar* (we do not come; you do not come; they do not come)

Sing: *almıyorum, almıyorsun, almıyor* (I do not take; you do not take; he/she/it does not take)

Pl: *almıyoruz, almıyorsunuz, almıyorlar* (we do not take; you do not take; they do not take)

Q.7.c) <u>Question</u>:

Sing: *Geliyor muyum? Geliyor musun? Geliyor mu?* (Am I coming? Are you coming? Is he/she/it coming?)

Pl: *Geliyor muyuz? Geliyor musunuz? Geliyorlar mı?* (Are we coming? Are you coming? Are they coming?)

Q.7.d) <u>Negative Question</u>:

Sing: *Gelmiyor muyum? Gelmiyor musun? Gelmiyor mu?* (Am I not coming? Are you not coming? Is he/she/it not coming?)

Pl: *Gelmiyor muyuz? Gelmiyor musunuz? Gelmiyorlar mı?* (Are we not coming? Are you not coming? Are they not coming?)

Q.8) **Simple Past, Active**: <u>I came</u> (Direct knowledge is indicated.)

Formula: verb stem + **-di/-dı/-dü/-du** (**-ti**, etc. after voiceless consonants) [= past marker] + Type II personal endings

Sing: *geldim, geldin, geldi* (I came; you came; he/she/it came)

Pl: *geldik, geldiniz, geldiler* (we came; you came; they came)

Negative: *gelmedim, gelmedin, gelmedi*, etc. (I didn't come; etc.)

Q.9) **"Miş" Past, Active**: <u>it is said that I came</u> (This tense, not found in English, indicates second-hand, or hearsay, knowledge.)

Formula: verb stem + **-miş/-mış/-müş/-muş** + Type I personal endings

Sing: *gelmişim, gelmişsin, gelmiş* (it is said that I came; etc.)

Pl: *gelmişiz, gelmişsiniz, gelmişler* (it is said that we came; etc.)

Negative: *gelmemişim, gelmemişsin, gelmemiş*, etc. (it is said that I didn't come; etc.)

Q.10) **"To Be."** In contrast with English, Turkish has no separate verb "to be." This concept is expressed by suffixes attached to nouns and adjectives. The suffixes closely resemble the Type I (for the present) and **-di/-dı/-dü/-du** + Type II (for the past) personal endings noted above in Q.5. In addition, in many tenses the verb **olmak** (to become) carries the meaning of "to be."

Q.10.a) <u>Present Sing</u>:
1st person ("I"): **-(y)im/-(y)ım/-(y)üm/-(y)um** [Use the **y** if the previous word ends with a vowel.]
2nd person ("you"): **-sin/-sın/-sün/-sun**
3rd person ("he/she/it"): **-dir/-dır/-dür/-dur** (written language; generally omitted when speaking). [Change **d** to **t** after an unvoiced consonant: **-tir**, etc.]

Present Pl:

1st person ("we"): **-(y)iz/-(y)ız/-(y)üz/-(y)uz**
[Use the **y** if the previous word ends with a vowel.]
2nd person ("you"): **-siniz/-sınız/-sünüz/-sunuz**
3rd person ("they"): **-dirler/-dırlar/-dürler/-durlar**
(written language; generally omitted when speaking).
[Change **d** to **t** after an unvoiced consonant: **-tirler**, etc.]

Examples: *Alman* (German); *Almanım* (I am German). *Amerikalı* (American person); *Amerikalıyım* (I am an American). *Öğrenci* (student); *öğrencisiniz* (you are a student).

Q.10.b) Past Sing:

1st person: **-dim/-dım/-düm/-dum**
2nd person: **-din/-dın/-dün/-dun**
3rd person: **-di/-dı/-dü/-du**

Past Pl:

1st person: **-dik/-dık/-dük/-duk**
2nd person: **-diniz/-dınız/-dünüz/-dunuz**
3rd person: **-diler/-dılar/-düler/-dular**. Also possible: **-lerdi/-lardı**.

Notes:
(a) Change **d** to **t** after an unvoiced consonant: **-tim**, etc.
(b) After a vowel, insert a **y** before the suffix: **-ydim**, etc.

Examples: *Öğrenciydim.* (I was a student.) *Hava soğuktu.* (The weather was cold.)

Q.10.c) <u>Negative of "to be"</u>: **değil** (not), to which the personal endings are attached.

Examples: *Öğrenci değilim.* (I am not a student.)
Öğrenci değildim. (I was not a student.)

Q.11) **"To Have."** In contrast with English, Turkish does not have a separate verb "to have." The concept is expressed by combining a noun + possessive ending with either the verb **var** (there is) or, for a negative, **yok** (there is not).

Examples: *araba* (car). **araba + m** (first person possessive suffix) + **var** → *Arabam var.* (I have a car.); *Arabam yok.* (I do not have a car.)
Question: *Arabanız var mı?* (Do you have a car?)
Answer: *Var* (Yes, I do) or: *Yok* (No, I do not).

<u>Past tense</u>: Add the past 3rd person endings of "to be" (see Section Q.10.b) to **var** or **yok**.

Examples: *Arabam vardı.* (I had a car.) *Arabanız yoktu.* (You did not have a car.)
Question: *Arabalarınız var mıydı?* (Did you have cars?)
Hayır, arabalarım yoktu. (No, I had no cars.)

Q.12) **Pluperfect, Active**: <u>I had come</u>. This tense is used to place events in more distant past time than either of the two past tenses already presented, Q.8 and Q.9. Despite its resemblance to Q.9, it indicates direct knowledge, not hearsay.

Formula: verb stem + **-miş/-mış/-müş/-muş** + **-ti/-tı/-tü/-tu** + Type II personal endings

Sing: *gelmiştim, gelmiştin, gelmişti* (I had come; you had come; he/she/it had come)

Pl: *gelmiştik, gelmiştiniz, gelmiştiler* (we had come; you had come; they had come)
Negative: *gelmemiştim*, etc. (I hadn't come; etc.)

Q.13) **Imperfect, Active**: I was going

Formula: verb stem + **-iyor/-ıyor** + **-du** + Type II personal endings

Sing: *geliyordum, geliyordun, geliyordu* (I was coming; you were coming; he/she/it was coming)
Pl: *geliyorduk, geliyordunuz, geliyordular/geliyorlardı* (we were coming; you were coming; they were coming)
Negative: *gelmiyordum*, etc. (I wasn't coming; etc.)

Q.14) **Future, Active**: I shall/will come

Formula: verb stem + **-ecek/-acak** [**-eceğ/-acağ**, when followed by a vowel] + Type I personal endings

Sing: *geleceğim, geleceksin, gelecek* (I shall come; you will come; he/she/it will come)
Pl: *geleceğiz, geleceksiniz, gelecekler* (we shall come; you will come; they will come)
Negative: *gelmeyeceğim*, etc. (I shall not come; etc.)
[Note: In this tense, the negative element **me** is separated from the tense marker **ecek** by a **y**.]

Q.15) **Future Past, Active**: I was about to come; I would come

Formula: verb stem + **-ecek/-acak** + **-ti/-tı** + Type II personal endings

Sing: *gelecektim, gelecektin, gelecekti* (I was about
        to come; you were about to come; he/she/it
        was about to come)
Pl: *gelecektik, gelecektiniz, gelecektiler* or *gelecek-
        lerdi* (we were about to come; you were about
        to come; they were about to come)
Negative: *gelmeyecektim*, etc. (I was not about to come;
          etc.)

Q.16) **"Aorist," Active.** In Turkish, this tense is
called **geniş zaman**, the "broad tense." This important
tense has no exact English equivalent. Its uses are many
and varied. In general, it indicates continuing, long-
lasting, or habitual activity. It is also used to express
polite requests and promises (but without firm commit-
ment) of future action. The negative is formed in a distinctive manner (see below).

Q.16.a) <u>Formulas (Positive)</u>:

(a) verb stem ending in a vowel + **r** + Type I personal
    endings
(b) Monosyllabic verb stem ending in a consonant +
    -er/-ar + Type I personal endings
    Exceptions to (b): Some verbs, mostly with a
    stem that ends with **l** or **r**, may have **-ir/-ır/-ür/
    -ur** as the aorist marker.
(c) Polysyllabic stem ending in a consonant + **-ir/-ır/
    -ür/-ur** + Type I personal endings

Sing: *gelirim, gelirsin, gelir* (I come; you come;
       he/she/it comes)
Pl: *geliriz, gelirsiniz, gelirler* (we come; you come;
       they come)

Q.16.b) <u>Negative</u>: Formed with **-mez** as the negative element; in the first person sing. and pl. this element is shortened to **-me**. In this tense, the negative element is stressed.

Sing: *gelmem, gelmezsin, gelmez* (I do not come; you do not come; he/she/it does not come); *almam, almazsın, almaz* (I do not take; etc.)
Pl: *gelmeyiz, gelmezsiniz, gelmezler* (we do not come; you do not come; they do not come); *almayız, almazsınız, almazlar* (we do not take; etc.)

Q.17) **Aorist Past, Active**: <u>I used to come; I would have come</u>

Formula: verb stem + aorist marker (as for Q.16) + **-di/-dı/-dü/-du** + Type II personal endings

Sing: *gelirdim, gelirdin, gelirdi* (I used to come; you used to come; he/she/it used to come)
Pl: *gelirdik, gelirdiniz, gelirdiler* or *gelirlerdi* (we used to come; etc.)

Negative: The element **-mez**, indicating the negative, is used in all persons, sing. and pl.
Sing: *gelmezdim, gelmezdin, gelmezdi* (I used not to come; etc.)
Pl: *gelmezdik, gelmezdiniz, gelmezdiler* or *gelmezlerdi* (we used not to come; etc.)

Q.18) **Imperative**: <u>Come! Let him come! Let them come</u>!

Formulas:
2nd person Sing: verb stem; no further ending
3rd person Sing: verb stem + **-sin/-sın/-sün/-sun**

2nd person Pl: verb stem + **-in(iz)/-ın(ız)/-ün(üz)/-un(uz)**
3rd person Pl: verb stem + **-sinler/-sınlar/-sünler/-sunlar**

Sing: *Gel!* (Come!) *Gelsin!* (Let him come!)
Pl: *Gelin!* or: *Geliniz!* (Come!) [The second form
       is more polite.]
       Gelsinler! (Let them come!)

Q.19) **Subjunctive**: <u>let me come; let us come</u>. The
first person forms are the most frequently seen; second
and third person forms, of rare application, are not
included here.

Formulas:
1st person Sing: verb stem + **-(y)eyim/-(y)ayım** [The **y** is
inserted when a verb stem ends in a vowel.]
Example: *geleyim* (let me come; I shall come)

1st person Pl: verb stem + **-(y)elim/-(y)alım**
Examples: *gelelim* (let's come); *gidelim* (let's go);
başlamak (to begin); *başlayalım* (let's begin)

Q.20) **"To be able; can."** This concept is expressed
by the element **-ebil/-abil** that is added to the verb stem.
The negative is expressed in a distinctive manner.

Formula (Positive): verb stem + **-(y)ebil/-(y)abil** + tense
marker + Type I or Type II (depending on the tense) personal endings
[Insert the **y** when the verb stem ends with a vowel.]

Examples: *gelebiliyorum* (I can come; present tense, as
in Q.7); *gelebildim* (I was able to come; simple past
tense, as in Q.8); *gelebilirim* (I can come; "aorist" tense,
as in Q.16).

Formula (Negative): verb stem + **-(y)eme/-(y)ama** + tense marker + Type I or Type II (depending on the tense) personal endings
[Insert the **y** when the verb stem ends with a vowel.]
In pronunciation, the first **e** or **a** is stressed.

Examples: *Gelemiyorum.* (I cannot come; present tense.)
<u>Note</u>: The second vowel of **(y)eme** changes to the **i** of the present tense marker **-iyor**. *Gelemedim.* (I could not come; simple past tense.)

<u>Aorist</u>:

Sing: *gelemem, gelemezsin, gelemez* (I cannot come; you cannot come; he/she/it cannot come)
Pl: *gelemeyiz, gelemezsiniz, gelemezler* (we cannot come; you cannot come; they cannot come)

Q.21) **Necessitative ("must")**: <u>I must come</u>. This concept can be expressed by placing the element **-meli/ -malı** after the verb stem and before Type I personal endings. This form is used primarily in a present and past tense.

Q.21.a) <u>Formula (Present)</u>: verb stem + **-meli/-malı** + Type I personal endings
Sing: *gelmeliyim, gelmelisin, gelmeli* (I must come/ I ought to come; etc.)
Pl: *gelmeliyiz, gelmelisiniz, gelmeliler* (we must come; etc.)

Q.21.b) <u>Negative</u>
Sing: *gelmemeliyim, gelmemelisin, gelmemeli* (I must not come; etc.)
Pl: *gelmemeliyiz, gelmemelisiniz, gelmemeliler* (we must not come; etc.)

Q.21.c) <u>Formula (Past)</u>: verb stem + **-meli/-malı** + **-ydi/-ydı** + Type II personal endings

Sing: *gelmeliydim, gelmeliydin, gelmeliydi* (I had to come/I should have come; etc.)

Pl: *gelmeliydik, gelmeliydiniz, gelmeliydiler* (we had to come; etc.)

Q.22) **Conditional ("if")**: "If' is expressed by the separate word **eğer**, but more importantly and indeed necessarily by the element **-se/-sa**.

Q.22.a) For the ordinary conditional, this **-se/-sa** element is placed after the tense marker and before the personal endings.

Formula: verb stem + tense marker + **-(y)se/-(y)sa** + personal endings

Examples:

Positive: *geliyorsam* (if I am coming; present tense);
geldiysem (if I came; simple past tense);
gelirseniz (if you come; aorist tense)

Negative: *gelmiyorsam* (if I am not coming);
gelmezseniz (if you are not coming; aorist)

Q.22.b) For a conditional that expresses a remote or unlikely condition, or a wish, the **-se/-sa** element is placed directly after the verb stem.

Formula (Present): verb stem + **-se/-sa** + Type II personal endings

Sing: *gelsem, gelsen, gelse* (if I were to come; if you were to come; if he/she/it were to come)

Pl: *gelsek, gelseniz, gelseler* (if we were to come; if you were to come; if they were to come)

Formula (Past): verb stem + **-se/-sa** + **-ydi/-ydı** + Type II personal endings

Sing: *gelseydim, gelseydin, gelseydi* (if [only] he had come; if [only] you had come; if [only] he/she/it had come)
Pl: *gelseydik, gelseydiniz, gelseydiler* or *gelse-lerdi* (if [only] we had come; if [only] you had come; if [only] they had come)

R) Impersonal Verbal Expressions

The following are common expressions in which a particular element is added to a verb stem; but this element is not itself followed by personal endings. The subject of the verbal expression is made clear elsewhere in the sentence. "He," as used in the list below, stands for the unexpressed subject.

a) **geldikten sonra** (after he comes)
b) **gelmeden önce** (before he comes)
c) **gelmeden** (without coming)
d) **gelince** (when he comes)
e) **gelinceye kadar** (until he comes)
f) **gelir gelmez** (as soon as he comes)
g) **gelerek** (by coming, by the action of coming)
h) **gelirken** (while coming)

S) Participles

Participles are crucial in Turkish, for they are the essential elements in complex sentences. They are used to express relative clauses and indirect speech. The differences here between Turkish and English syntax are striking. Literal translations, comical and awkward though they seem, are offered as helpful tools for mastering Turkish usage. The four main participles, with some examples of their use, are as follows:

S.1) Present Participle

Formula: verb stem + **-(y)en/-(y)an**
[Insert the **y** when the verb stem ends with a vowel.]

Examples: *gelen* (coming; the one who comes); *alan* (taking; the one who takes); *gelen adam* (the man who is coming); *alan adam* (the man who is taking)

S.2) **Future Participle**: This participle indicates future action.

Formula: verb stem + **-(y)ecek/-(y)acak**

Example: *gelecek adam* (the man who will come; *lit.* the will-be-coming man)

Note: This participle can take possessive endings. The **k** changes to **ğ** when followed by a vowel.

Examples: *geleceğimi söyledi* (he said that I would come; *lit.* my will-be-coming he said); *okuyacağınız kitaplar* (the books that you will read; *lit.* your will-be-reading books)

S.3) **-miş Participle**: This participle denotes action completed. It does not indicate information learned indirectly, although in form it resembles the "miş" past tense (Q.9).

Formula: verb stem + **-miş/-mış/-müş/-muş**

Examples: *pişmiş yemek* (the food that has been cooked); *gelmiş adam* (the man who has come; *lit.* the having-come man)

S.4) *-dik* **Participle**: This participle also denotes completed action.

Formula: verb stem + **-dik/-dık/-dük/-duk**
[Replace **d** with **t** when the verb stem ends with an unvoiced consonant.]

Note: In contrast with the **-miş** participle, the **-dik** participle can take possessive endings. The **k** changes to **ğ** when followed by a vowel.

Examples: *gördüğüm turistik yerler* (the touristic sites that I have seen; *lit.* the my-having-seen touristic sites). *Ahmet Bey beğendiğiniz kitabı aldı.* (Ahmet Bey bought the book that you liked; *lit.* Ahmet Bey the your-having-liked book bought.) *Ayşe Hanım İstanbul'a gitmediği için, dersi salı günü yapabileceğiz.* (Because Ayşe Hanım did not go to Istanbul, we will be able to hold the class on Tuesday; *lit.* Ayşe Hanım Istanbul-to having-not-gone because, the lesson Tuesday we will be able to hold.)

Note: With this last construction, the **-diği için** construction, the subject does NOT take a possessive ending.

T) Verbal Nouns

Of the several types of verbal nouns, the **-me/-ma** verbal noun is particularly useful for beginners to know, for the two common uses indicated below. As in Section S, on

Participles, literal translations are offered as devices for learning the sentence patterns.

Formula: verb stem + **-me/-ma**. Possessive endings can then be added.

Examples: *gelme* (coming); *bekleme* (waiting); *gelmem* (my coming)

a) With **lazım** (necessity), or the conjugated verb **gerekmek**, to indicate necessity: *Gitmem lazım.* (I must go; *lit.* my going is a necessity.) *Kitapları okumamız gerekiyor.* (We must read the books; *lit.* the books our-reading is necessary.)

b) In indirect commands: *Annem bakkala gitmemizi söyledi.* ([My] Mother told us to go to the grocery store; *lit.* mother-my grocery store-to our-going said/told.)

TURKISH-ENGLISH DICTIONARY

*When the English speaker's instinct is unlikely to produce the correct suffix governed by a particular word, the suffix is supplied, with both front and back vowel versions. The suffixes are: **-e/-a**, **-den/-dan**, **-i/-ı**, **-i/-ı/-ü/-u**, **-in/-ın/-ün/-un**, **-le/-la**.

A

abla *n.* elder sister
abone *n.* subscription
acaba I wonder if...?
acele *adj./n.* urgent; hurry, haste
acc *adj./n.* bitter; hot *(spicy)*; pain
acıkmak *v.* to feel hungry
aç *adj.* hungry
açık *adj.* open; clear; light *(color)*
açıklamak *v.* to explain
açmak *v.* to open; to turn on, start *(a machine)*
ad *n.* name
ada *n.* island
adam *n.* man
adres *n.* address
aferin *interj.* bravo! well done!
affetmet *v.* to pardon, excuse, forgive
afiyet olsun to your health, bon appétit!
ağabey *n.* elder brother
ağaç *n.* tree
ağır *adj.* heavy; serious
ağız *n.* mouth
ağlamak *v.* to cry *(weep)*

ağrımak *v.* to ache, hurt
ağustos *n.* August
aile *n.* family
ait *postp.* belonging to, concerning *(-e/-a)*
ak *adj.* white, clean
akciğer *n.* lung(s)
akıllı *adj.* intelligent, clever
akmak *v.* to drip, flow
akraba *n.* relative *(family)*
akrep *n.* scorpion
akşam *n.* evening
alan *n.* plain; space
alaturka *adj./adv.* in the Turkish fashion
alçak *adj.* low, vile, base
alerji *n.* allergy
alın *n.* forehead
alışmak *v.* to be accustomed to, used to *(-e/-a)*
alışveriş *n.* shopping, buying and selling
alkış *n.* applause
alkol *n.* alcohol
Allah *n.* God
almak *v.* to take; to buy
Alman *adj./n.* German
Almanca *n.* German language
Almanya *n.* Germany
alt *adj./n.* lower; lower part, underside
altı *n.* six
altın *n.* gold
altmış *n.* sixty
ama *conj.* but
amaç *n.* aim, target
amca *n.* paternal uncle
Amerika Birleşik Devletleri (ABD) *n.* United States of
      America (USA)
an *n.* moment, instant
ana *n.* mother

anahtar *n.* key
anayasa *n.* constitution *(law)*
ancak *conj.* however, but
anlamak *v.* to understand
anlatmak *v.* to explain
anne *n.* mother
apartman *n.* apartment building
aptal *adj.* stupid
ara *n.* interval; intermission; relations *(between people)*
araba *n.* car, automobile; cart, carriage
aralık *n.* December
aramak *v.* to seek, look for
arka *n.* back; back side; the space behind
arkadaş *n.* friend
arkeoloji *n.* archaeology
armut *n.* pear
arzu *n.* wish, desire
asansör *n.* elevator, lift
asker *n.* soldier
aşağı *adv./n.* below, down; downstairs; the lower
        part, bottom
at *n.* horse
ata *n.* father; old man
ateş *n.* fire; fever
atmak *v.* to throw, throw away
Avrupa *n.* Europe
avukat *n.* lawyer, solicitor
ay *n.* month; moon
ayak *n.* foot, leg
ayakkabı *n.* shoe
ayı *n.* bear *(animal)*
ayıp *n.* shameful behavior, disgrace
ayırmak *v.* to separate, divide
ayırtmak *v.* to set aside, reserve
ayna *n.* mirror

aynı *adj.* same

ayran *n.* a drink of yogurt, water, and a pinch of salt

ayrı *adj.* separate

ayrılmak *v.* to separate oneself from; to leave *(-den/-dan)*

ayva *n.* quince

az *adv.* little *(amount)*, few; seldom

azalmak *v.* to diminish, be reduced

B

baba *n.* father

bacak *n.* leg

bacanak *n.* brother-in-law *(husband of one's wife's sister)*

bagaj *n.* luggage, suitcase

bağlı *postp.* connected to, tied to *(-e/-a)*

bahar *n.* spring *(season)*

bahçe *n.* garden

bahsetmek *v.* to discuss, speak about *(-den/-dan)*

bakan *n.* minister *(government)*

bakanlık *n.* ministry *(government)*

bakım *n.* upkeep, attention; point of view

bakkal *n.* grocer

bakmak *v.* to look at *(-e/-a)*

bal *n.* honey

balık *n.* fish

balkon *n.* balcony

banka *n.* bank *(financial)*

banyo *n.* bath

bardak *n.* glass *(drinking)*

barış *n.* peace

basmak *v.* to step on, press on

baş *n.* head, top; beginning

başarmak *v.* to succeed in *(-i/-ı)*

başbakan *n.* prime minister

başka *adj.* other, another

başkent *n.* capital city
başlamak *v.* to begin *(-e/-a)*
başvurmak *v.* to apply, make an application
batı *n.* west
bay *n.* gentleman; Mr.
bayan *n.* lady; Mrs., Miss, Ms. *(= marital status not specified)*
bayılmak *v.* to faint
bayrak *n.* flag
bayram *n.* religious festival, holiday
bazen, bazan *adv.* sometimes
bazı *adj.* some, a few
bebek *n.* baby; doll
bedava *adj.* free, for nothing
beğenmek *v.* to like, approve, admire
bekâr *adj./n.* unmarried; bachelor
bekçi *n.* watchman, guard
beklemek *v.* to await, wait for *(-i/-ı)*
belediye *n.* municipality
belge *n.* document, certificate
belki *adv.* maybe, perhaps
belli *adj.* clear, evident
ben *pron.* I
benzemek *v.* to resemble *(-e/-a)*
benzin *n.* gasoline, petrol
beraber *adv.* together
berber *n.* barber
beri *postp.* since *(-den/-dan)*
beş *n.* five
bey *n.* gentleman; Mr. *(used after the first name)*; husband
beyaz *adj.* white
beyefendi *n.* sir
bezelye *n.* pea, peas
bıçak *n.* knife
bırakmak *v.* to leave, quit
bıyık *n.* moustache

biber *n.* pepper
biftek *n.* beefsteak
bilek *n.* wrist
bilet *n.* ticket
bilezik *n.* bracelet
bilgi *n.* knowledge, information
bilgisayar *n.* computer
bilmek *v.* to know
bin *n.* thousand
bina *n.* building
binmek *v.* to get on; to mount, ride *(-e/-a)*
bir *n.* one
bira *n.* beer
biraz *adj.* a little
birdenbire *adv.* suddenly
birkaç *adj.* a few, some
birleşik *adj.* united
bisiklet *n.* bicycle
bitirmek *v. tr.* to finish
bitmek *v. intr.* to come to an end, be finished
biz *pron.* we
Bizans *adj./n.* Byzantine; Byzantium
boğaz *n.* throat; strait
Boğaziçi *n.* Bosphorus
bol *adj.* abundant, plentiful; loose-fitting
borç *n.* debt; obligation
boru *n.* pipe, tube
boş *adj.* empty
boy *n.* size; height
boya *n.* paint; dye
boyun *n.* neck
boza *n.* drink made of slightly fermented millet
bozmak *v.* to spoil; to damage; to upset *(plans, stomach)*; to change *(money)*
bozuk *adj.* broken, spoiled, destroyed
böcek *n.* insect

bölge *n.* region, district, zone

bölüm *n.* division, portion; chapter; department *(academic)*

börek *n.* flaky pastry filled with meat, cheese, or
     vegetables

böyle *adv.* so, thus, such, in this way

bu *adj./pron.* this

buçuk *adj.* and a half *(after numerals)*

bugün *n.* today

bulaşık *n.* dirty dishes

bulgur *n.* boiled and pounded wheat

bulmak *v.* to find

buluşmak *v.* to meet, come together

bulut *n.* cloud

burada *adv.* here

burun *n.* nose; headland, cape; point, tip; beak, bill

buyurun! *v. interj.* Please come in! Please sit down!
     Please have some!

buz *n.* ice

buzdolabı *n.* refrigerator, icebox

bülbül *n.* nightingale

büro *n.* office

bütün *adj.* whole, entire, all

büyük *adj.* big, large; great; older person

büyükanne *n.* paternal grandmother

büyükbaba *n.* grandfather *(maternal and paternal)*

büyükelçilik *n.* embassy

C

cacık *n.* a cold soup of yogurt, chopped cucumber,
     and garlic

cadde *n.* street, avenue

cam *n.* glass *(material)*

cami *n.* mosque

can *n.* soul; life; vigor, vitality

canım *n.* my dear, darling, precious; dear fellow
canlı *adj.* living, alive; lively
cehennem *n.* hell
ceket *n.* sports coat, jacket of a suit
cenaze *n.* funeral
cennet *n.* paradise, heaven
cep *n.* pocket
cevap vermek *v.* to answer *(-e/-a)*
ceviz *n.* walnut
ceza *n.* penalty, fine, punishment
ciddi *adj.* serious
ciğer *n.* liver; lung(s)
cuma *n.* Friday
cumartesi *n.* Saturday
cumhurbaşkanı *n.* president of the republic
cumhuriyet *n.* republic
cümle *n.* sentence *(grammar)*
cüzdan *n.* wallet, billfold; booklet *(official document)*

Ç

çabuk *adv.* fast, quick
çadır *n.* tent
çağ *n.* period, age, era, time
çağdaş *adj.* contemporary
çağırmak *v.* to call, invite, summon
çakıl *n.* pebble, gravel
çalışmak *v.* to work
çalmak *v.* to steal; to play *(a musical instrument)*; to ring
    (a bell, a doorbell)
çam *n.* pine tree
çamaşır *n.* laundry, dirty laundry
çamur *n.* mud
çanta *n.* bag, sack
çare *n.* solution *(to a problem)*, remedy

çarpmak *v.* to strike, collide with, knock against *(-e/-a)*

çarşaf *n.* sheet, bedsheet

çarşamba *n.* Wednesday

çarşı *n.* bazaar, group of shops

çatal *n.* fork

çay *n.* tea

çekiç *n.* hammer

çekmek *v.* to pull; to take *(a photograph)*

çelik *n.* steel

çengel *n.* hook

çeşit *n.* variety, kind, sort

çeşme *n.* fountain

çevre *n.* environment, surroundings

çeyrek *n.* quarter hour

çıkarmak *v.* to remove; to extract; to take off *(clothing, hat)*

çıkış *n.* exit

çıkmak *v.* to go out, come out

çıplak *adj.* naked, bare

çiçek *n.* flower

çiftlik *n.* farm

çiğnemek *v.* to chew

çikolata *n.* chocolate

çilek *n.* strawberry

çimento *n.* cement

çirkin *adj.* ugly

çivi *n.* nail *(metal)*

çizgi *n.* line; stripe

çoban *n.* shepherd

çocuk *n.* child

çok *adv.* very; much, many; often

çorap *n.* sock *(clothing)*

çorba *n.* soup

çöp *n.* garbage, trash

çünkü *conj.* because

çürük *adj.* rotten, decayed

D

dağ *n.* mountain
daha *adj./adv.* more; -er *(comparative)*; until now,
    yet, still
dahil *adj.* including, included; interior
daire *n.* apartment, flat
dakika *n.* minute *(time)*
dalga *n.* wave *(of water; of heat or cold)*
danışma *n.* information
dans *n.* dance, dancing
dans etmek *v.* to dance
dar *adj.* narrow, tight
davet etmek *v.* to invite
davul *n.* drum *(musical instrument)*
dayanaklı *adj.* durable, sturdy; tough *(person)*
dayı *n.* maternal uncle, mother's brother
dede *n.* grandfather *(maternal and paternal)*
defa *n.* time, turn
define *n.* treasure
defter *n.* notebook; register
değer *n.* value, worth
değil *adv.* not
değişmek *v.* to change
deli *adj.* crazy
delik *n.* hole
demek *v.* to say
demir *n.* iron *(metal)*
denemek *v.* to try, test
deniz *adj./n.* naval, marine; sea, ocean
deprem *n.* earthquake
derece *n.* degree
dereotu *n.* dill
deri *n.* skin, hide; leather
derin *adj.* deep
ders *n.* class, lesson; course

desteklemek *v.* to support, prop up
devam etmek *v.* to continue; to attend
deve *n.* camel
devlet *n.* state, government
dış *adj./n.* foreign; external; outside, exterior
dışarı *adj./adv.* out; outside
diğer *adj./n.* other; the other
dikkat *n./interj.* careful attention; Be careful! Look out!
dil *n.* tongue; language
dilemek *v.* to wish (for); to request
dilim *n.* slice, piece
din *n.* religion
dinlemek *v.* to listen to *(-i/-ı/-ü/-u)*
dinlenmek *v.* to rest
diş *n.* tooth
diz *n.* knee
doğa *n.* nature
doğmak *v.* to be born
doğru *adj./adv.* true; straight
doğu *n.* east
doğum *n.* birth
doksan *n.* ninety
doktor *n.* doctor
dokunmak *v.* to touch *(-e/-a)*
dokuz *n.* nine
dolap *n.* closet; wardrobe; cupboard
dolaşmak *v.* to walk around, stroll; wander
dolma *adj.* filled, stuffed
dolmuş *n.* shared taxi
dolu *adj.* full, filled
domates *n.* tomato
domuz *n.* pig
dondurma *n.* ice cream
dost *adj./n.* friendly; friend
dosya *n.* file, dossier
doymak *v.* to eat one's fill, be full *(food)*

dökmek *v.* to pour, pour out; to spill
döner *n.* meat roasted on a vertical spit
dönmek *v.* to turn, rotate; to return
dört *n.* four
döviz *n.* foreign currency or money
dudak *n.* lip
duman *n.* smoke; fumes; haze
durak *n.* stop *(bus, train, etc.)*
durmak *v.* to stop; to last, continue to exist
durum *n.* state, condition; situation
duş *n.* shower
duvar *n.* wall
duygu *n.* feeling; emotion; sensation
duymak *v.* to hear; to feel, perceive
düğün *n.* wedding; wedding feast
dükkân *n.* shop
dün *n.* yesterday
dünya *n.* world, the earth
düşman *n.* enemy
düşmek *v.* to fall, fall down
düşünmek *v.* to think of, think about *(-i/-ı/-ü/-u)*
düz *adj.* flat; level; smooth; even; straight
düzeltmek *v.* to correct; to repair; to straighten out

E

ebru *adj.* marbled *(paper)*
eczane *n.* pharmacy, drugstore
edebiyat *n.* literature
efendi *adj./n.* polite, courteous *(person)*; gentleman
efendim *interj.* Yes, sir/madam! *(when someone has called your name)*; I beg your pardon?; Hello? *(telephone)*
efsane *n.* legend, tale
Ege *n.* Aegean, Aegean Sea

eğer *conj.* if

eğitim *n.* education

eğlenmek *v.* to have fun, have a good time

ehliyet / ehliyetname *n.* driver's license

ek *adj./n.* extra; supplement, appendix

ekim *n.* October; sowing

ekmek *n.* bread

eksik *adj.* lacking, deficient

ekşi *adj.* sour

el *n.* hand

elbette *adv.* certainly, surely

elbise *n.* dress *(woman's)*

elçi *n.* ambassador, envoy

elektrik *adj./n.* electric, electrical; electricity

elli *n.* fifty

elma *n.* apple

emanet *adj./n.* entrusted to *(-e/-a)*; checkroom for baggage

emekli *adj./n.* retired *(worker, etc.)*

emin *adj.* sure, certain

emlak *n.* real estate

emniyet *n.* security, safety

en *adj.* most *(superlative)*

enerji *n.* energy

enginar *n.* artichoke

enişte *n.* aunt's husband; brother-in-law *(sister's husband)*

erik *n.* plum

erkek *n.* man; male

erken *adj./adv.* early

ertesi *adj.* the next, the following *(day, week)*

eser *n.* work of art; sign, trace

eski *adj.* old *(thing)*, ancient; former

eş *n.* husband; wife; match, equal

eşek *n.* donkey

eşya *n.* furnishings; belongings

et *n.* meat, flesh

etek *n.* skirt *(dress)*

etki *n.* effect, impression

etmek *v.* to do *(auxiliary verb)*
ev *n.* house, home
evet *adv.* yes
evlenmek *v.* to get married; to marry *(-le/-la)*
evli *adj.* married
evvel *postp.* before *(-den/-dan)*
eylül *n.* September
ezmek *v.* to crush, mash

F

fabrika *n.* factory
faiz *n.* interest *(banking)*
fakat *conj.* but
fakir *adj.* poor, impoverished, destitute
fare *n.* mouse
fark *n.* difference
fasulye *n.* bean, beans
fayda *n.* use, usefulness, benefit
fazla *adj./adv.* too; too much; too many
felaket *n.* disaster, catastrophe
fen *n.* natural sciences
fena *adj.* bad
fındık *n.* hazelnut, filbert
fırça *n.* brush *(painting, sweeping)*
fırın *n.* oven; bakery; kiln
fırsat *n.* opportunity, chance
fırtına *n.* storm
fıstık *n.* peanut; pistachio
fikir *n.* thought, idea, opinion
film (filim) *n.* film *(for a camera)*; movie
fincan *n.* coffee cup; teacup
fiş *n.* plug *(on an electrical cord)*; slip of paper;
        shopping receipt

fiyat *n.* price
fotoğraf *n.* photograph
fotoğraf çekmek *v.* to photograph, take a photo

G

galiba *adv.* probably
garaj *n.* garage; bus station
garip *adj.* strange, curious
garson *n.* waiter
gazete *n.* newspaper
gazino *n.* big nightclub; outdoor café
gece *n.* night
geç *adj.* late, delayed
geçen *adj.* past, last
geçmek *v.* to pass
gelecek *adj./n.* coming; future; the future
gelin *n.* bride
gelişmek *v.* to develop, mature
gelmek *v.* to come
gemi *n.* ship, boat
genç *adj./n.* young; young person
gene *adv.* again
genellikle *adv.* generally
geniş *adj.* wide, broad
gerçek *adj./n.* real, true; reality
gerekmek *v.* to be necessary
geri *adv.* back, backward, behind
getirmek *v.* to bring
gevşek *adj.* loose, slack
gezmek *v.* to tour; to walk around; to take a (pleasure) trip
gibi *postp.* like
gidiş *n.* going; departure
giriş *n.* entry, entrance; going in; introduction

girmek *v.* to enter, go in(to) *(-e/-a)*

gişe *n.* ticket window; box office *(theater)*

gitmek *v.* to go

giyinmek *v.* to dress oneself

giymek *v.* to wear, put on

gizli *adj.* secret, hidden

göbek *n.* navel; belly; traffic circle

göçmek *v.* to migrate, emigrate, immigrate

göğüs *n.* chest, breast

gök *n.* sky, heaven

göl *n.* lake

gölge *n.* shadow, shade

gömlek *n.* shirt

göndermek *v.* to send

göre *postp.* according to *(-e/-a)*

görev *n.* duty; job, function

görmek *v.* to see

görüşmek *v.* to talk (with), visit (with) *(-le/-la)*

göstermek *v.* to show, point out

götürmek *v.* to carry, transport, take away

göz *n.* eye

gözlük *n.* (eye)glasses

gram *n.* gram

greyfurt *n.* grapefruit

gurur *n.* pride

güç *n.* power, strength

gül *n.* rose

gülmek *v.* to laugh

gümrük *n.* customs bureau

gümüş *n.* silver

gün *n.* day

günah *n.* sin

günaydın *interj.* Good morning!

gündüz *adv./n.* in the daytime; daytime

güneş *n.* sun

güney *n.* south
gürültü *n.* noise
güzel *adj.* beautiful, pretty

H

haber *n.* news
hac *n.* hajj, pilgrimage to Mecca; pilgrimage
haç *n.* cross, crucifix
hafif *adj.* light *(weight)*; mild, light
hafta *n.* week
hak *n.* justice, fairness; one's right
hakaret etmek *v.* to insult
hakikaten *adv.* really, truly
haklı *adj.* right, just
hal *n.* situation, condition
hala *n.* paternal aunt, father's sister
hâlâ *adv.* still, yet
halı *n.* rug, carpet
halk *n.* people, folk, populace
hamam *n.* Turkish bath, public bath
hamamböceği *n.* cockroach
hamile *adj.* pregnant
han *n.* large commercial building, caravansaray; khan
    (Ottoman and Asian title)
hangi *adj./pron.* which
hanım *n.* lady; wife; Mrs./Ms./Miss *(used after a
    first name)*
hanımefendi *n.* lady, madam
hapishane *n.* prison, jail
harabe *n.* ruins, remains
hardal *n.* mustard
hareket *n.* movement, motion; departure
hariç *adj.* except for; excluded; outside
harika *adj.* wonderful, marvelous

harita *n.* map
hassas *adj.* sensitive
hasta *adj./n.* sick, ill; sick person, patient
hastane *n.* hospital
hatırlamak *v.* to remember, recall
hava *n.* air; atmosphere; weather
havalimanı *n.* airport
havuç *n.* carrot
hayat *n.* life
haydi *interj.* Come on!
hayır *adv.* no; *n.* prosperity
hayvan *n.* animal
hazır *adj.* ready, prepared
hazine *n.* treasure; treasury
haziran *n.* June
hedef *n.* target, goal
hediye *n.* gift, present
hem ... hem ... *conj.* both ... and ...
hemen *adv.* immediately, right now
henüz *adv.* yet *(in negative sentences)*
hep *adj.* all
her *adj.* every, each
herhalde *adv.* surely, certainly
herkes *pron.* everyone, everybody
hesap *n.* bill, check *(restaurant, etc.)*; calculation
heyecan *n.* excitement
heykel *n.* statue, sculpture
hırsız *n.* thief
hız *n.* speed
hiç *adv./pron.* never; not at all; nothing
hikâye *n.* story, tale
hindi *n.* turkey *(bird)*
hissetmek *v.* to feel, sense, perceive
hoca *n.* Muslim cleric; teacher
hoş *adj.* pleasant, agreeable
Hristiyan *adj./n.* Christian
hudut *n.* border, frontier

hükümet *n.* government
hürriyet *n.* freedom, liberty

I

ıhlamur *n.* linden tea; linden tree
ısınmak *v.* to warm up, get warm
ıslak *adj.* wet
ısmarlamak *v.* to order *(something)*
ıspanak *n.* spinach
ışık *n.* light
ızgara *adj./n.* grilled; grill *(for cooking)*

İ

iade etmek *v.* to return, give back, send back
iç *n.* the interior, the inside
içecek *adj./n.* drinkable; beverage, drink
içeri *n.* inside, interior
için *postp.* for
içki *n.* alcoholic beverage
içmek *v.* to drink; to smoke; to eat *(soup)*
idare *n.* management, administration
iftar *n.* meal at sundown during Ramazan
ihtimal *n.* probability
ihtiyaç *n.* necessity
ihtiyar *n.* old person, senior
ikamet *n.* residence
iki *n.* two
ikram *n.* treating, offering *(food, drink, etc. to a guest)*
ilaç *n.* medicine; disinfectant; pesticide
ile *postp.* with, together with
ileri *adj./n.* advanced; fast *(clock, watch)*; forward
        part, front

ilginç *adj.* interesting

ilk *adj.* first

ilkbahar *n.* spring *(season)*

ilköğretim *n.* elementary education

imam *n.* Muslim cleric

imkân *n.* possibility

imparatorluk *n.* empire

imza *n.* signature

imzalamak *v.* to sign, autograph

inanmak *v.* to believe *(-e/-a)*

ince *adj.* slender, slim; fine, delicate

inci *n.* pearl

incir *n.* fig

indirim *n.* reduction *(in price)*, discount, sale

İngiliz *adj./n.* English

İngilizce *n.* English language

İngiltere *n.* England

inmek *v.* to go down, come down, get off *(bus, airplane, train, etc.) (-den/-dan)*

insan *n.* person, someone, human being

inşallah *interj.* God willing; I hope that …

ip *n.* rope, string, cord

ipek *n.* silk

iptal etmek *v.* to cancel

ise *conj.* as for; however; if

ishal *n.* diarrhea

isim *n.* name; title *(book, etc.)*

iskele *n.* dock, wharf, pier

iskemle *n.* chair *(without arms)*; stool

istasyon *n.* station; railway station

istek *n.* wish, desire

istemek *v.* to want, wish

istifa etmek *v.* to resign *(from a position)*

istiklal *n.* independence

iş *n.* work; job, employment; occupation; business

işçi *n.* worker, workman

işitmek *v.* to hear
işte *adv./interj.* as you see; Look! Here!
itfaiye *n.* fire department
ithal etmek *v.* to import
itmek *v.* to push
iyi *adj./adv.* good; well
izin *n.* permission; leave *(of absence)*
izlemek *v.* to observe, watch, view; to follow

K

kabak *n.* zucchini, squash; pumpkin
kabuk *n.* shell; crust; bark; rind, peel; scab *(wound)*
kabul etmek *v.* to accept; to agree
kaç *adv.* How many? How much is it?
kaçmak *v.* to escape; to run away; to slip away
kadar *adv./postp.* as ... as ...; as much as; until, up
        to *(-e/-a)*
kadın *n.* woman
kafa *n.* head; mental attitude
kâğıt *n.* paper, piece of paper
kahvaltı *n.* breakfast
kahve *n.* coffee; café
kahverengi *adj./n.* brown
kalabalık *adj./n.* crowded; crowd; clutter
kalamar *n.* squid
kaldırım *n.* sidewalk
kaldırmak *v.* to lift up, raise; to remove
kale *n.* fort, fortress, citadel
kalem *n.* pen, pencil
kalın *adj.* thick
kalkmak *v.* to get up; to stand up; to go up; to depart
        (train, bus, etc.)
kalmak *v.* to remain, be left; to stay
kalorifer *n.* heating system; heating unit; furnace

kalp *n.* heart

kambiyo *n.* foreign exchange *(currency)*

kan *n.* blood

Kanada *n.* Canada

Kanadalı *adj./n.* Canadian

kanat *n.* wing; fin *(fish)*; leaf *(door, window)*

kanun *n.* law, statute

kapalı *adj.* closed, shut; covered; roofed

kapamak *v.* to close, shut, cover up

kapı *n.* door; gate

kapıcı *n.* doorkeeper; maintenance man *(for a building)*

kar yağmak *v.* to snow

kara *adj./n.* black; swarthy; terrestrial; dry land

karakol *n.* police station

karanlık *adj./n.* dark; darkness, the dark

karar *n.* decision

kardeş *n.* brother; sister; sibling

karı *n.* wife

karın *n.* stomach, belly, abdomen

karınca *n.* ant

karışık *adj.* mixed; confused, disorganized; complex

karpuz *n.* watermelon

karşı *adj./postp.* opposite, facing, against *(-e/-a)*

karşılamak *v.* to go to meet, to meet

kas *n.* muscle

kasap *n.* butcher; butcher shop

kasım *n.* November

kaşar *n.* a yellow cheese made of sheep's milk

kaşık *n.* spoon

kat *n.* story, floor *(building)*; layer, fold

kavak *n.* poplar tree

kavga *n.* quarrel; brawl; struggle

kavun *n.* muskmelon, cantaloupe, melon

kayak *n.* ski; skiing

kaybetmek *v.* to lose

kaygan *adj.* slippery, slick

kayıt *n.* enrollment, registration
kaymak *n.* cream; *v.* to slip, slide
kaynak *n.* source; spring *(water)*
kaza *n.* accident
kazanmak *v.* to earn; to win; to acquire
kazı *n.* excavation
kebap *n.* dish with meat or other food in small pieces
keçi *n.* goat
kedi *n.* cat
kel *adj.* bald
kelebek *n.* butterfly
kelime *n.* word
keman *n.* violin
kemik *n.* bone
kenar *n.* edge, border, shore, margin
kendi *n./pron.* self, oneself; own; he, she
kent *n.* city
kere *n.* time; **iki kere** two times
kereviz *n.* celery root, celeriac, celery
kesmek *v.* to cut
keten *n.* linen, flax
keyif *n.* pleasure, feeling of well-being
Kıbrıs *n.* Cyprus
kılıç *n.* sword; swordfish
kına *n.* henna
kırk *n.* forty
kırmak *v.* to break
kırmızı *adj./n.* red
kısa *adj.* short
kısım *n.* part, portion, section
kısmet *n.* destiny, fortune
kış *n.* winter
kıyma *n.* ground meat
kız *n.* girl; daughter
kızartma *adj.* fried
kızıl *adj.* red

kızmak *v.* to get angry
kibrit *n.* match *(for fire)*
kilim *n.* a type of woven, pileless rug
kilise *n.* church
kilo *n.* kilo, kilogram
kilometre *n.* kilometer
kim *pron.* who; whoever
kimlik *n.* identity; identity card
kimse *pron.* someone, anybody *(in a question)*; nobody
    (with a negative verb)
kimyon *n.* cumin
kira *n.* renting; rent
kiraz *n.* cherry
kirli *adj.* dirty
kişi *n.* person
kitap *n.* book
koca *adj./n.* very big, grand; husband
koku *n.* smell, scent, odor; perfume
kol *n.* arm; limb; branch; division
kolay *adj.* easy, simple
koltuk *n.* armchair; armpit
komşu *n.* neighbor
konferans *n.* lecture; colloquium, conference
konser *n.* concert
konsolos *n.* consul *(diplomat)*
konu *n.* subject, topic
konuşma *n.* talk, lecture, public speech; talking
konuşmak *v.* to talk, speak
kopya *n.* copy
korkmak *v.* to fear, be afraid (of) *(-den/-dan)*
korumak *v.* to protect, defend, watch over
koşmak *v.* to run
kova *n.* bucket
koymak *v.* to put, place
koyu *adj.* dark *(color)*; thick *(liquid)*
koyun *n.* sheep

köfte *n.* ground meat patty; meatball
kömür *n.* coal; charcoal
köpek *n.* dog
köprü *n.* bridge
kör *adj./n.* blind, blind person
köşe *n.* corner
kötü *adj.* bad; evil; poor in quality
köy *n.* village
köylü *n.* villager; peasant
kral *n.* king
kraliçe *n.* queen
kubbe *n.* dome
kulak *n.* ear
kule *n.* tower
kullanmak *v.* to use; to drive *(a car)*
kum *n.* sand
kumaş *n.* cloth
kumpir *n.* baked potato with toppings
kural *n.* rule, regulation
kurban *n.* sacrifice, sacrificial animal
Kurban Bayramı *n.* Feast of the Sacrifice
kurmak *v.* to establish; to set up *(something)*; to set
  (the table)
kurşun *n.* lead *(metal)*; bullet
kurtarmak *v.* to save, rescue
kuru *adj.* dry, dried
kuruş *n.* cent *(100 kuruş per lira)*
kuş *n.* bird
kuşbaşı *n.* meat cut in small chunks
kutlamak *v.* to congratulate; to celebrate
kutu *n.* box; can
kuvvet *n.* strength, power
kuyruk *n.* tail
kuyu *n.* well; pit
kuzey *n.* north
kuzu *n.* lamb

küçük *adj.* small, little
kül *n.* ash
küpe *n.* earring
kürek *n.* shovel
kürk *n.* fur
kütüphane *n.* library

L

lahit *n.* sarcophagus
lahmacun *n.* flat bread with meat and tomato topping
lamba *n.* lamp
lastik *n.* rubber *(material)*; tire; rubber band
lavabo *n.* washroom; washbasin
lazım *adj.* necessary
leke *n.* stain, spot
levha *n.* signboard, sign
leylek *n.* stork
lezzetli *adj.* delicious, tasty
liman *n.* harbor, port
limon *n.* lemon
lira *n.* lira *(Turkish monetary unit)*
lise *n.* high school
lokanta *n.* restaurant
lokum *n.* Turkish delight *(a candy)*
lütfen *interj.* please

M

maalesef *adv./interj.* unfortunately; I regret to say
maaş *n.* salary
maden *n.* metal; mineral; mine
mağara *n.* cave, cavern
mahalle *n.* neighborhood, city district

makale *n.* article *(newspaper, magazine)*
makas *n.* scissors, shears
makina *n.* machine
mal *n.* property, possessions; wealth
mana *n.* meaning, significance
manav *n.* seller of fruits and vegetables; store where
    fruits and vegetables are sold
mantar *n.* mushroom; cork
manzara *n.* view, panorama
mart *n.* March
marul *n.* romaine lettuce
masa *n.* table, desk
masraf *n.* expense
maşallah *interj.* Wonderful! May God preserve him/her
    from evil!
mavi *adj./n.* blue
maydanoz *n.* parsley
mayıs *n.* May
mecburi *adj.* compulsory, required
meclis *n.* parliament; assembly, council
mektup *n.* letter
memleket *n.* country; one's home region or town
memnun *adj.* pleased, happy
memur *n.* civil servant, bureaucrat
mendil *n.* handkerchief
merak *n.* curiosity; great interest; anxiety, worry
mercimek *n.* lentil
merdiven *n.* stairs, staircase; ladder
merhaba *interj.* hello, hi
merkez *n.* center, central; headquarters
mesela for example
meslek *n.* profession
meşgul *adj.* busy, occupied (with)
meşhur *adj.* famous, renowned
meşrubat *pl.n.* beverages
metre *n.* meter

mevsim *n.* season

meydan *n.* public square; wide open space

meyve *n.* fruit

mezar *n.* tomb, grave

mezun olmak *v.* to graduate *(from school, college, etc.)*

mısır *n.* corn

Mısır *n.* Egypt

mide *n.* stomach, belly

midye *n.* mussel

miktar *n.* quantity, amount; portion

millet *n.* nation

milli *adj.* national

milyar *n.* billion

milyon *n.* million

mimar *n.* architect

minare *n.* minaret

miras *n.* inheritance, heritage, legacy

misafir *n.* guest, visitor

mola *n.* rest, pause, break

muhasebeci *n.* accountant, bookkeeper

mum *n.* candle; wax

Musevi *adj./n.* Jewish; Jew

musluk *n.* faucet, tap, spigot

mutfak *n.* kitchen

mutlu *adj.* happy; lucky

müdür *n.* director, head, manager; headmaster/
headmistress

mühendis *n.* engineer

mühim *adj.* important

mümkün *adj.* possible

müracaat *n.* application; reception or information desk

müsaade *n.* permission

Müslüman *adj./n.* Muslim, Islamic

müşteri *n.* customer, client

müze *n.* museum

müzik *n.* music

N

nakliyat *n.* transport, shipping
namaz *n.* Muslim ritual prayer
nane *n.* mint, peppermint
nasıl *adv.* how?
ne *pron.* what?
ne zaman *adv.* when?
neden *adv./n.*. why?; cause; reason
nehir *n.* river
nerede *adv.* where?
nereden *adv.* from where?
nereli *adj.* What country/region/city (are you) from?
nereye *adv.* to where?
niçin *adv.* why?
nihayet *adv./n.* at last, finally; end, conclusion
nisan *n.* April
nişanlı *adj./n.* engaged to be married; fiancé(e)
niye *adv.* why?
nohut *n.* chickpea, garbanzo
nokta *n.* point, dot; period *(punctuation)*; place
normal *adj.* normal
nöbetçi *n.* person on duty; watchman, sentry
numara *n.* number; shoe size
nüfus *n.* population, inhabitants

O

o *pron.* he, she, it; that, those
ocak *n.* January; stove; furnace; quarry
oda *n.* room
odun *n.* firewood
ofis *n.* office
oğul *n.* son
okul *n.* school

okumak *v.* to read; to study
olay *n.* event, incident
olmak *v.* to become, happen, be
omuz *n.* shoulder
on *n.* ten
orada *adv.* there, in that place
ordu *n.* army
orman *n.* forest
orta *adj./n.* middle
oruç tutmak *v.* to fast
Osmanlı *adj./n.* Ottoman
otel *n.* hotel
otobüs *n.* bus
otogar *n.* bus station
oturmak *v.* to sit, sit down; to live *(in a place)*
otuz *n.* thirty
ova *n.* plain
oynamak *v.* to play; to perform *(a play)*
oyun *n.* game; play *(theater)*
oyuncu *n.* actor, actress; player *(of a game)*

Ö

öbür *adj.* the other *(person/thing)*
ödemek *v.* to pay
ödev *n.* homework, assignment; duty
ödünç *adj.* borrowed, loaned, on loan
öğle *n.* noon, midday
öğrenci *n.* student
öğrenmek *v.* to learn
öğretmek *v.* to teach
öğretmen *n.* teacher
ölçü *n.* measurement, measure, unit of measure
öldürmek *v.* to kill

ölmek *v.* to die
ölü *adj./n.* dead; dead person or thing
ölüm *n.* death
ön *n.* front, front part
önce *adv./postp.* first, at first; ago; before *(-den/-dan)*
önem *n.* importance
önemli *adj.* important
öpmek *v.* to kiss
örnek *n.* example
örümcek *n.* spider
öyle *adv.* thus, so, in that manner
öz *adj.* pure, genuine
özel *adj.* private, personal; special, exceptional
özet *n.* summary
özgür *adj.* free
özür dilemek *v.* to beg (one's) pardon, apologize

P

pahalı *adj.* expensive
paket *n.* package
palamut *n.* tuna, bonito
palto *n.* overcoat
pamuk *n.* cotton
pansiyon *n.* pension, guesthouse
pantolon *n.* pants, trousers
papaz *n.* priest, minister, pastor
para *n.* money
parça *n.* piece; fragment, bit
park *n.* park; parking lot
parlak *adj.* bright, shining, brilliant
parmak *n.* finger; toe
pasaport *n.* passport
paslanmak *v.* to rust, tarnish, corrode

pasta *n.* cake
pastane *n.* pastry shop
pastırma *n.* smoked, dried beef
patates *n.* potato
patlama *n.* explosion
patlıcan *n.* eggplant
paylaşmak *v.* to share
pazar *n.* market; bazaar; Sunday
pazartesi *n.* Monday
peçete *n.* napkin
peki *adv.* all right, okay, very well
pekmez *n.* molasses-like fruit syrup
pembe *adj./n.* pink
pencere *n.* window
perde *n.* curtain
perşembe *n.* Thursday
peynir *n.* cheese
pınar *n.* spring *(water)*
pide *n.* slightly leavened flat bread
pil *n.* battery
pilav *n.* rice pilaf; cooked rice
piliç *n.* chicken, young chicken
pirinç *n.* rice *(uncooked grains)*
pis *adj.* dirty, foul
pişirmek *v.* to cook; to fire *(ceramics, bricks)*
pişmek *v.* to be cooked; to be fired *(ceramics)*
piyango *n.* lottery
plaj *n.* beach
plaka *n.* license plate
planlamak *v.* to plan
polis *n.* police
portakal *n.* orange *(fruit)*
posta *n.* mail; postal service
postane *n.* post office
profesör *n.* professor
pul *n.* postage stamp
pusula *n.* compass *(for direction)*

R

radyo *n.* radio
raf *n.* shelf
rağmen *postp.* in spite of *(-e/-a)*
rahat *adj./n.* comfort, ease, peace and quiet; comfortable
rahatsız *adj.* uncomfortable; unwell
rakı *n.* raki, ouzo *(anise-flavored alcoholic drink)*
Ramazan *n.* Ramadan *(ninth month in the Muslim lunar calendar, when Muslims fast from sunrise to sunset)*
randevu *n.* appointment
reçel *n.* jam, preserves
reddetmek *v.* to refuse, decline
rehber *n.* guide; tourist guidebook; telephone directory
renk *n.* color
resim *n.* picture, drawing, painting
resmi *adj.* formal, official
ressam *n.* artist, painter
rezalet *n.* disgrace, scandal, outrage
rica *n.* request
ruh *n.* soul, spirit
Rum *adj./n.* Greek *(of Cyprus or Turkey)*
rüşvet *n.* bribe
rüya *n.* dream
rüya görmek *v.* to dream
rüzgâr *n.* wind, breeze

S

saat *n.* hour; time of day; clock, watch
sabah *n.* morning
sabun *n.* soap
saç *n.* hair *(on a person's head)*
sade *adj.* plain, simple
sağ *adj./n.* healthy, well; right, right side

sağır *adj./n.* deaf, deaf person
sağlık *n.* health
saha *n.* field, area; playing field *(sports)*
sahil *n.* coast, shore
sakal *n.* beard
sakin *adj.* calm, tranquil
saklamak *v.* to hide
saksı *n.* flowerpot
salata *n.* salad, lettuce
salı *n.* Tuesday
salon *n.* living room; large room
sanat *n.* art
sanatçı *n.* artist
sandalye *n.* chair *(armless)*
sanki *conj.* as if
sanmak *v.* to think, suppose
sap *n.* handle
sapmak *v.* to turn to; to enter *(a road)*
saray *n.* palace
sarhoş *adj.* drunk
sarı *adj.* yellow
sarmısak *n.* garlic
satıcı *n.* seller, salesman, saleswoman
satın almak *v.* to buy
satmak *v.* to sell
satranç *n.* chess
savaş *n.* war, fight
sayfa *n.* page *(book, newspaper, etc.)*
sayın *adj.* Dear ... *(letter heading)*; esteemed
saymak *v.* to count
sebep *n.* cause, reason
sebze *n.* vegetable
seçim *n.* election
seçmek *v.* to choose
sefer *n.* journey, trip; time, occasion
sekiz *n.* eight
sekreter *n.* secretary

seksen *n.* eighty

sel *n.* flood

selam *n.* greeting, hello

sen *pron.* you *(sing. informal)*

sene *n.* year

serbest *adj.* free, open, unrestricted

sergi *n.* exhibition, display

serin *adj.* cool; chilly

sert *adj.* hard, tough

ses *n.* sound, noise; voice

sevgili *adj.* beloved, dear; Dear ... *(heading of a friendly letter)*

sevinç *n.* joy

sevinmek *v.* to feel happy, feel glad

sevmek *v.* to love, like

seyahat *n.* trip, journey

seyretmek *v.* to watch, look at *(-i/-ı/-ü/-u)*

sıcak *adj.* hot

sıfır *n.* zero

sıkışmak *v.* to be crowded, placed close together

sınav *n.* test, examination

sınıf *n.* class; category; classroom

sınır *n.* border, frontier

sıra *n.* row, line; sequence; turn

sırt *n.* back *(body)*

sıvı *n.* liquid, fluid

sigara *n.* cigarette

sigorta *n.* insurance; fuse *(electric)*

silah *n.* weapon

silmek *v.* to wipe

simit *n.* ring-shaped roll covered with sesame seeds

sinek *n.* fly

sinema *n.* movie theater

sirke *n.* vinegar

sis *n.* fog, mist, haze

sivrisinek *n.* mosquito

siyah *adj./n.* black

siz *pron.* you *(sing. formal; pl.)*
soğan *n.* onion
soğuk *adj.* cold *(temperature)*
sokak *n.* street
sol *adj./n.* left, left side
son *adj./n.* end; the last
sonbahar *n.* autumn, fall
sonra *adv./postp.* later, afterwards; after *(-den/-dan)*
sonraki *adj.* next, subsequent, following
sormak *v.* to ask
soru *n.* question
sorun *n.* problem
soyadı *n.* surname, family name
sökmek *v.* to dismantle, tear down, take apart, uproot
söndürücü *n.* fire extinguisher
söylemek *v.* to say, tell; to sing
söz *n.* word; remark, statement; promise
söz vermek *v.* to promise *(-e/-a)*
sözlük *n.* dictionary
spor *n.* sport, sports
su *n.* water
sucuk *n.* a type of sausage
susmak *v.* to be silent
sünger *n.* sponge
sünnet *n.* circumcision
sürmek *v.* to drive; to spread, rub (something) on; to take
  (a certain amount of time)
süt *n.* milk
süzgeç *n.* strainer, filter

Ş

şair *n.* poet
şaka *n.* joke
şans *n.* luck
şapka *n.* hat

şarap *n.* wine
şarkı *n.* song
şart *n.* condition, stipulation
şaşırmak *v.* to be surprised, bewildered
şaşmak *v.* to be amazed at, astonished at *(-e/-a)*
şehir *n.* city, town
şeker *n.* sugar; candy
şekil *n.* shape, form; way, manner
şemsiye *n.* umbrella, parasol, beach umbrella
şeref *n.* honor
şey *n.* thing
şiir *n.* poem, poetry
şikâyet *n.* complaint
şimdi *adv.* now
şimşek *n.* flash of lightning
şirket *n.* company, firm
şiş *n.* skewer, spit
şişe *n.* bottle
şişman *adj.* fat
şoför *n.* driver *(of a car or bus)*; chauffeur
şöyle *adv.* thus, thusly, in this/that way
şu *adj./pron.* this, that
şubat *n.* February
şüphe *n.* suspicion, doubt, uncertainty

T

taahhütlü *adj.* registered *(letter)*
tabak *n.* plate, dish; saucer
tabaka *n.* layer, stratum
taban *n.* floor, base; sole *(foot, shoe)*
tabanca *n.* pistol, revolver, gun
tabii *adj./adv.* natural; of course, naturally
taç *n.* crown
tahin *n.* sesame seed paste
tahmin etmek *v.* to guess, estimate

tahta *adj./n.* wooden; board, plank; wood
takip etmek *v.* to follow
taksi *n.* taxi
takvim *n.* calendar
tam *adj.* whole, full, complete
tamam *adj./adv.* correct; okay
tane *n.* kernel, grain; item, piece *(with this meaning, usually left untranslated in English)*
tanımak *v.* to recognize, be acquainted with, know
tanışmak *v.* to make the acquaintance of *(-le/-la)*
tanrı *n.* god, deity
taraf *n.* side
tarih *n.* date *(calendar)*; history
tarla *n.* field *(agricultural)*
tartmak *v.* to weigh
taş *n.* stone, rock
taşımak *v.* to carry, transport; to bear, support
taşınmak *v.* to move *(to a new residence or place of business)*
tatil *n.* holiday, vacation
tatlı *adj.* sweet; pleasant, agreeable
tava *adj./n.* fried; frying pan
tavan *n.* ceiling
tavla *n.* backgammon
tavsiye *n.* recommendation
tavşan *n.* rabbit, hare
tavuk *n.* chicken, hen
taze *adj.* fresh, young, new
tebrik *n.* congratulation
tebrik etmek *v.* to congratulate
tecavüz *n.* aggression; molestation, rape
tecrübe *n.* experience; experiment
tedavi *n.* treatment *(medical)*, therapy; cure
tehlike *n.* danger
tek *adj./n.* single, sole, alone; a single thing
tekerlek *n.* wheel

tekrar *adv./n.* again; repetition
tekrarlamak *v.* to repeat
tel *n.* wire, thread
telefon *n.* telephone
telefon etmek *v.* to telephone *(-e/-a)*
televizyon *n.* television
tembel *adj.* lazy
temiz *adj.* clean
temizlemek *v.* to clean
temmuz *n.* July
temsilci *n.* representative, agent
tencere *n.* cooking pot *(lidded)*
tepe *n.* hill; top, top part
tepsi *n.* tray; large, shallow, open baking dish
ter *n.* sweat, perspiration
terbiyeli *adj.* polite, well-mannered
tercih *n.* preference
tercüman *n.* interpreter
tercüme *n.* translation
tereyağı *n.* butter
terlik *n.* slipper
ters *n.* reverse; opposite side, end
terzi *n.* tailor; dressmaker
tesis *n.* facility; establishment; institution
teslim *n.* delivering, handing over; submission, yielding
teşekkür *n.* thanking, thanks
Teşekkür ederim Thank you
teşekkür etmek *v.* to thank
teyze *n.* maternal aunt
tıkalı *adj.* stopped up, clogged
tıraş *n.* shave, shaving
ticaret *n.* trade, commerce
titiz *adj.* meticulous, hard to please, picky, fastidious
tiyatro *n.* theater
tonbalığı *n.* tuna fish
top *n.* ball; cannon

toplamak *v.* to collect, gather
toplantı *n.* meeting
toprak *n.* earth, soil, dirt
torba *n.* bag, sack
tornavida *n.* screwdriver
torun *n.* grandchild
toz *n.* dust; powder
tören *n.* ceremony; rite
tren *n.* train, railroad
tuhaf *adj.* strange, curious, odd
Tuna *n.* Danube
tunç *n.* bronze
turist *n.* tourist
turizm *n.* tourism
turşu *n.* pickle
tutkal *n.* glue
tutmak *v.* to hold, take hold of
tuvalet *n.* toilet, lavatory, W.C.
tuz *n.* salt
tuzak *n.* trap, snare
tuzlu *adj.* salty
tüfek *n.* rifle
tüm *adj.* all of, all
tüp *n.* tube; cylinder *(for bottled gas)*
Türk *adj./n.* Turkish; Turk
Türkçe *n.* Turkish language
Türkiye *n.* Turkey

U

ucuz *adj.* cheap
uçak *n.* airplane
uçmak *v.* to fly
ufak *adj.* tiny, small, minor
uğramak *v.* to stop by, drop in on *(-e/-a)*

ulus *n.* nation
ummak *v.* to hope
un *n.* flour
unutmak *v.* to forget
usta *n.* master *(of a trade/craft)*; skilled or master workman
uyanmak *v. intr.* to wake up, awaken
uygun *adj.* suitable, convenient, appropriate *(-e/-a)*
uyku *n.* sleep; sleepiness
uyumak *v.* to sleep
uzak *adj./adv.* distant, far
uzman *n.* expert
uzun *adj.* long; tall

Ü

ücret *n.* fee, cost; wage
üç *n.* three
ülke *n.* country *(state)*
ümit *n.* hope
üniversite *n.* university
ünlü *adj.* famous
üretim *n.* production
üst *n.* upper surface, top
ütü *n.* iron *(for ironing clothes)*
üye *n.* member *(of a group)*
üzere *adv.* on the point of, just about to
üzeri *n.* upper surface, top
üzülmek *v.* to be upset, distressed *(-e/-a)*
üzüm *n.* grape

V

vakit *n.* time
vali *n.* governor of a province

vapur *n.* steamship
var *v.* there is, there are
varış *n.* arrival
varmak *v.* to arrive
vatan *n.* native country, fatherland, motherland
vatandaşlık *n.* citizenship
vazgeçmek *v.* to decide not to (do sthg.), give up
      (-den/-dan)
ve *conj.* and
vergi *n.* tax
vermek *v.* to give
vesaire (v.s.) et cetera (etc.)
veya *conj.* or
vezne *n.* cashier's office/window
vida *n.* screw
vişne *n.* sour cherry
vurmak *v.* to hit, strike; to shoot; to kill
vücut *n.* body *(of a person/animal)*

W

WC *n.* W.C. *(water closet)*, toilet

Y

ya *interj.* Oh...!
ya ... ya ... *conj.* either ... or ...
yabancı *n.* foreigner, stranger
yağ *n.* oil; grease; fat
yağmak *v.* to rain
yağmur *n.* rain
Yahudi *adj./n.* Jewish; Jew
yahut *conj.* or
yakın *adv.* near *(-e/-a)*

yakıt *n.* fuel *(for heating)*

yakmak *v.* to burn; to set fire to, ignite

yalan *n.* lie, falsehood

yalı *n.* waterside house/mansion; shore, beach

yalnız *adj./adv.* alone; lonely; only; *conj.* but, however

yan *n.* side

yanak *n.* cheek

yangın *n.* fire *(destructive)*

yani *interj.* that is to say, I mean, namely

yankı *n.* echo

yanlış *adj./n.* wrong; mistake, error

yanmak *v. intr.* to burn, be on fire; to be burned; to get
      sunburned; to get suntanned

yapışmak *v. intr.* to stick, adhere, cling (to)

yapmak *v.* to make; to do; to build

yaprak *n.* leaf; grape leaf; sheet *(of dough, pastry)*

yara *n.* wound; open sore; injury

yarar *n.* benefit, advantage

yardım *n.* help, aid

yarı *n.* half (of the ...)

yarım *adj./n.* half

yarın *n.* tomorrow

yarışma *n.* contest, competition; racing

yasak *adj./n.* prohibited, forbidden; prohibition

yastık *n.* pillow; cushion

yaş *n.* age *(of a person)*; tears *(in the eyes)*

yaşamak *v.* to live; to live in, inhabit

yaşlı *adj.* old *(person)*, elderly

yatak *n.* bed

yatırım *n.* investment

yatmak *v.* to go to bed; to be in bed

yavaş *adj.* slow, quiet; gentle; *adv.* slowly

yaya *n.* pedestrian

yaygın *adj.* widespread

yayınevi *n.* publishing house, press

yayla *n.* plateau; mountain pasture

yaz *n.* summer

yazar *n.* writer, author

yazı *n.* writing; piece of writing, written article; handwriting

yazık *n.* pity, shame

yazmak *v.* to write

yedek *n.* spare; standby, something held in reserve

yedi *n.* seven

yeğen *n.* nephew; niece

yemek *n.* food; *v.* to eat

yenge *n.* uncle's wife; sister-in-law *(brother's wife)*

yeni *adj.* new

yenmek *v.* to defeat, beat, overcome; to be eaten

yer *n.* place

yeraltı *adj.* underground

yerinde *prep.* instead of *(-in/-ın/-ün/-un)*

yeşil *adj.* green

yetişmek *v.* to catch, make, be in time for *(-e/-a)*

yetmek *v.* to be enough

yetmiş *n.* seventy

yıkamak *v.* to wash; to launder

yıkanmak *v.* to be washed; to wash oneself

yıl *n.* year

yıldırım *n.* flash of lightning, thunderbolt

yıldız *n.* star

yırtmak *v.* to tear, rip

yine *adv.* again

yirmi *n.* twenty

yoğun *adj.* intense, intensive; dense, thick

yoğurt *n.* yogurt

yok *v.* there is not, there are not

yoksa *conj.* or

yol *n.* road, way, route

yolcu *n.* passenger, traveler

yolculuk *n.* trip, journey, voyage

yollamak *v.* to send

yorgan *n.* quilt
yorgun *adj.* tired
yorulmak *v.* to tire, be/get tired
yön *n.* direction
yönetici *n.* manager, administrator
yönetim *n.* management, administration
yufka *n.* phyllo, thin sheet of dough
yukarı *n.* upper part; upstairs
yulaf *n.* oat
yumurta *n.* egg
yumuşak *adj.* soft
Yunanistan *n.* Greece
yurt *n.* homeland, native country; national territory;
      home; dormitory
yuvarlak *adj.* round, circular, spherical
yüksek *adj.* high; superior
yükselmek *v.* to rise, ascend; to increase; to advance
yün *n.* wool
yürek *n.* heart
yürümek *v.* to walk
yüz *n.* hundred; face
yüzde *n.* percent, percentage
yüzmek *v.* to swim
yüzük *n.* ring *(worn on a finger)*
yüzyıl *n.* century

Z

zafer *n.* victory
zahmet *n.* trouble, difficulty, inconvenience
zam *n.* price increase; wage increase
zaman *n.* time
zarar *n.* damage, injury, harm
zarf *n.* envelope
zaten *adv.* anyway, in any case; in fact

zavallı *adj.* poor, miserable, pitiful
zayıf *adj.* weak; thin, scrawny
zehir *n.* poison
zemin *n.* ground floor; ground
zenci *n.* black (person)
zengin *adj.* rich
zeytin *n.* olive
zil *n.* doorbell; cymbal; finger cymbal
zincir *n.* chain
ziyaret *n.* visit
zor *adj./n.* difficult; difficulty; obligation; physical force
zümrüt *n.* emerald

ENGLISH-TURKISH DICTIONARY

A

abundant *adj.* bol
accident *n.* kaza
according to *prep.* göre *(-e/-a)*
accountant *n.* muhasebeci
(be) accustomed to *v.* alışmak *(-e/-a)*
ache *v.* ağrımak
actor *n.* oyuncu
actress *n.* oyuncu
address *n.* adres
administration *n.* yönetim
administrator *n.* yönetici
advanced *adj.* ileri
advantageous *adj.* yararlı
Aegean (Sea) *n.* Ege
(be) afraid *v.* korkmak *(-den/-dan)*
after *prep.* sonra *(-den/-dan)*
again *adv.* gene, tekrar, yine
age *n.* çağ, devir *(period)*; yaş *(of a person)*
aggression *n.* tecavüz
ago *adj./adv.* evvel, önce
aim *n.* amaç, hedef
air *n.* hava
airplane *n.* uçak
airport *n.* havaalanı, havalimanı
alcohol *n.* alkol
alcoholic beverage *n.* içki
alive *adj.* canlı
all *adj.* hep, tüm
all right *adv.* peki, tamam

allergy *n.* alerji
alone *adj.* yalnız
(be) amazed (at) *v.* şaşmak *(-e/-a)*
ambassador *n.* elçi
America *n.* Amerika
American *adj.* Amerikan; *n.* Amerikalı
and *conj.* ve
(be) angry *v.* kızmak *(with, at: -e/a)*
animal *n.* hayvan
another *adj.* başka
answer *v.* cevap vermek *(-e/-a)*
ant *n.* karınca
anyone *pron.* kimse
anyway *adv.* zaten
apartment *n.* daire
apartment building *n.* apartman
applause *n.* alkış
apple *n.* elma
application *n.* müracaat
apply, make an application *v.* başvurmak
appointment *n.* randevu
April *n.* nisan
Arab(ian) *adj./n.* Arap
archaeologist *n.* arkeolog
archaeology *n.* arkeoloji
architect *n.* mimar
arm *n.* kol
armchair *n.* koltuk
Armenian *adj./n.* Ermeni
armpit *n.* koltuk
army *n.* ordu
arrival *n.* varış, geliş
arrive *v.* varmak
art *n.* sanat
artichoke *n.* enginar
article *(magazine, newspaper)* *n.* makale

artist *n.* sanatçı
as ... as ... *adv.* kadar
as for *conj.* ise
as if *conj.* sanki
ashtray *n.* kül tablası
ask *v.* sormak
attack *n.* saldırı
attention *n.* dikkat
August *n.* ağustos
aunt *n.* hala *(paternal)*, teyze *(maternal)*
author *n.* yazar
await *v.* beklemek *(-i/-ı)*

B

baby *n.* bebek
bachelor *n.* bekâr
back *adj./adv.* geri; *n.* arka; sırt *(body)*
backgammon *n.* tavla
backward *adv.* geri
bad *adj.* fena, kötü
bag *n.* çanta, torba
balcony *n.* balkon
bald *adj.* kel
ball *n.* top
bandage *n.* sargı; yarabandı *(small)*
bank *(financial)* *n.* banka
bar *n.* bar
barber *n.* berber, erkek ku(v)aförü
bare *adj.* çıplak
bath *n.* banyo
battery *n.* pil
bazaar *n.* çarşı, pazar
be *v.* olmak; **there is/are** var; **there is/are not** yok (See
    also Grammar Section Q.10)

beach *n.* plaj
bean(s) *n.* fasulye
bear *(animal)* *n.* ayı
beard *n.* sakal
beautiful *adj.* güzel
because *conj.* çünkü
become *v.* olmak
bed *n.* yatak
beefsteak *n.* biftek
beer *n.* bira
before *prep.* evvel, önce *(-den/-dan)*
beg (one's) pardon *v.* özür dilemek **(for:** *-den/-dan)*
begin *v.* başlamak *(-e/-a)*
believe *v.* inanmak *(-e/-a)*
belong *v.* ait olmak *(-e/-a)*
belonging to *adj.* ait *(-e/-a)*
belongings *n.* eşya
beloved *adj./n.* sevgili
below *adv./prep.* aşağı
beverages *pl.n.* meşrubat
bicycle *n.* bisiklet
big *adj.* büyük
bill *(restaurant, etc.)* *n.* hesap
billion *n.* milyar
bird *n.* kuş
birth *n.* doğum
bitter *adj.* acı
black *adj./n.* siyah, kara
black (person) *n.* zenci
Black Sea *n.* Karadeniz
blind *adj./n.* kör
blood *n.* kan
blue *adj./n.* mavi
board *n.* tahta
body *n.* vücut
bon appétit afiyet olsun

bone *n.* kemik
book *n.* kitap
border *(country)* *n.* hudut, sınır
(be) born *v.* doğmak
borrow *v.* ödünç almak
Bosphorus *n.* Boğaziçi
both ... and ... *conj.* hem ... hem ...
bottle *n.* şişe
bracelet *n.* bilezik
bravo *interj.* aferin!
bread *n.* ekmek
break *v.* kırmak
breakfast *n.* kahvaltı
bribe *n.* rüşvet
bride *n.* gelin
bridge *n.* köprü
bright *adj.* parlak
bring *v.* getirmek
broken *adj.* bozuk
bronze *n.* tunç
brother *n.* kardeş
brother-in-law *n.* bacanak *(husband of one's wife's*
sister); enişte *(sister's husband)*
brown *adj./n.* kahverengi
brush *(painting, sweeping)* *n.* fırça
bucket *n.* kova
building *n.* bina
Bulgaria *n.* Bulgaristan
bullet *n.* kurşun
burn *v. intr.* yanmak; *v. tr.* yakmak
bus *n.* otobüs
bus station *n.* garaj, otogar
busy *adj.* meşgul
but *conj.* ama, fakat
butcher *n.* kasap
butter *n.* tereyağı

butterfly *n.* kelebek
buy *v.* almak, satın almak
Byzantine *adj.* Bizans

C

cake *n.* pasta
calendar *n.* takvim
call *v.* çağırmak
calm *adj.* sakin
camel *n.* deve
(tin) can *n.* kutu, teneke
can *v.* -ebilmek
Canada *n.* Kanada
cancellation *n.* iptal
candle *n.* mum
candy *n.* bonbon, şeker
capital city *n.* başkent
car *n.* araba
carpet *n.* halı
carrot *n.* havuç
carry *v.* götürmek, taşımak
cart *n.* araba
cashier's window *n.* vezne
cat *n.* kedi
catch *v.* tutmak, yakalamak; yetişmek *(bus, etc.)*
cause *n.* sebep
cave *n.* mağara
ceiling *n.* tavan
celebrate *v.* kutlamak
celery root *n.* kereviz
cement *n.* çimento
center *n.* merkez
century *n.* yüzyıl
ceremony *n.* tören

chain *n.* zincir

chair *n.* iskemle, sandalye

change *v.* değişmek

change (**money**) *v.* bozmak

change (**one's**) **mind** *v.* vazgeçmek *(-den/-dan)*

charcoal *n.* mangal kömürü

cheap *adj.* ucuz

checkroom *(baggage)* *n.* emanet

cheek *n.* yanak

cheese *n.* peynir

cherry *n.* kiraz, vişne

chess *n.* satranç

chest *(breast)* *n.* göğüs

chew *v.* çiğnemek

chicken *n.* piliç, tavuk

chickpea *n.* nohut

child *n.* çocuk

chocolate *n.* çikolata

choose *v.* seçmek

Christian *adj./n.* Hristiyan

church *n.* kilise

cigarette *n.* sigara

circle *n.* daire

circumcision *n.* sünnet

citizenship *n.* vatandaşlık

city *n.* kent, şehir

civil servant *n.* memur

class *n.* ders *(lesson, course)*; sınıf *(school class, grade;
        classroom)*; çeşit *(kind, sort)*

clean *adj.* temiz; *v.* temizlemek

clear *adj.* açık *(empty, cloudless)*; belli *(evident, obvious)*

clever *adj.* akıllı

clock *n.* saat

clogged *adj.* tıkalı

close *v.* kapamak

closed *adj.* kapalı

closet *n.* dolap
cloth *n.* kumaş
cloud *n.* bulut
coal *n.* kömür
cockroach *n.* hamamböceği
coffee *n.* kahve
coffee cup *n.* fincan
cold *adj.* soğuk *(temperature)*; *n.* nezle *(illness)*
collect *v.* toplamak
color *n.* renk
come *v.* gelmek
Come on! *interj.* Haydi!
comfortable *adj.* rahat
commerce *n.* ticaret
company *(business) n.* şirket
compass *n.* pergel *(drawing)*; pusula *(for direction)*
complaint *n.* şikâyet
compulsory *adj.* mecburi
computer *n.* bilgisayar
concert *n.* konser
condition *n.* hal; şart *(stipulation)*
confused *adj.* karışık
congratulate *v.* kutlamak, tebrik etmek
Congratulations! *interj.* Tebrikler! Tebrik ederim!
connected to *adj.* bağlı *(-e/-a)*
constitution *(law) n.* anayasa
consul *n.* konsolos
consulate *n.* konsolosluk
contemporary *adj.* çağdaş
contest *n.* yarışma
continue *v.* devam etmek *(-e/-a)*
convenient *adj.* uygun
cook *n.* aşçı; *v. intr.* pişmek; *v. tr.* pişirmek
cooking pot *n.* tencere
cool *adj.* serin
copy *n.* kopya

cork *n.* mantar
corkscrew *n.* tirbuşon
corn *n.* mısır
corner *n.* köşe
correct *v.* düzeltmek
cotton *n.* pamuk
count *v.* saymak
country *n.* memleket, ülke
crazy *adj.* deli
cream *n.* kaymak, krema
cross *n.* haç *(crucifix)*; *v.* geçmek *(i.e. cross the street)*
crowded *adj.* kalabalık
crown *n.* taç
crush *v.* ezmek
cry *(weep)* *v.* ağlamak
cumin *n.* kimyon
cure *n.* tedavi
curiosity *n.* merak
(foreign) currency *n.* döviz
curtain *n.* perde
cushion *n.* yastık
customer *n.* müşteri
customs (bureau) *n.* gümrük
cut *n.* kesik, kesme; *v.* kesmek
cymbal *n.* zil
Cyprus *n.* Kıbrıs

D

damage *n.* zarar
dance *n.* dans; *v.* dans etmek
danger *n.* tehlike
Danube *n.* Tuna
dark *adj.* karanlık; koyu *(color)*
darkness *n.* karanlık

darling *n.* canım
date *(calendar) n.* tarih
daughter *n.* kız
day *n.* gün
daytime *n.* gündüz
dead *adj./n.* ölü
deaf *adj./n.* sağır
Dear *(letter heading) adj.* Sayın *(formal)*; Sevgili *(informal)*
death *n.* ölüm
debt *n.* borç
December *n.* aralık
decide *v.* kararlaştırmak; karar vermek *(-e/-a)*
decision *n.* karar
deep *adj.* derin
defeat *v.* yenmek
degree *n.* derece
delivery *n.* teslim
departure *n.* gidiş
describe *v.* tarif etmek
desire *n.* arzu
dessert *n.* tatlı
destiny *n.* kısmet, kader
develop *v.* gelişmek
diarrhea *n.* ishal
dictionary *n.* sözlük
die *v.* ölmek
difference *n.* fark
difficult *adj.* zor
dill *n.* dereotu
diminish *v.* azalmak
direction *n.* yön
director *n.* müdür; rejisör *(theater, movies)*
dirty *adj.* kirli, pis
dirty dishes *n.* bulaşık
disaster *n.* felaket
disgusting *adj.* iğrenç

dish *n.* tabak
dismantle *v.* sökmek
distant *adj.* uzak
do *v.* yapmak
doctor *n.* doktor
document *n.* belge
dog *n.* köpek
dome *n.* kubbe
donkey *n.* eşek
door *n.* kapı
doorbell *n.* zil
dormitory *n.* yurt
down *adv.* aşağı
dream *n.* rüya; *v.* rüya görmek
dress *(woman's)* *n.* elbise
dress oneself *v.* giyinmek
drink *n.* içecek; içki *(alcoholic)*; *v.* içmek
drip *v.* akmak
drive *v.* kullanmak *(a car)*, sürmek *(a vehicle)*
driver *n.* şoför
driver's license *n.* ehliyet, ehliyetname
drum *n.* davul
drunk *adj.* sarhoş
dry *adj.* kuru
durable *adj.* dayanaklı
dust *n.* toz
duty *n.* görev, ödev
dye *n.* boya

E

each *adj.* her
ear *n.* kulak
early *adj./adv.* erken
earn *v.* kazanmak

earring *n.* küpe
earth *n.* toprak *(dirt, soil)*; dünya *(world)*
earthquake *n.* deprem
east *n.* doğu
easy *adj.* kolay
eat *v.* yemek
eat one's fill *v.* doymak
echo *n.* yankı
edge *n.* kenar
education *n.* eğitim
effect *n.* etki
egg *n.* yumurta
eggplant *n.* patlıcan
Egypt *n.* Mısır
eight *n.* sekiz
eighty *n.* seksen
either ... or ... *conj.* ya ... ya ...
elder brother *n.* ağabey
elder sister *n.* abla
election *n.* seçim
electric *adj.* elektrik
electricity *n.* elektrik
elementary education *n.* ilköğretim
elevator *n.* asansör
embassy *n.* büyükelçilik
emerald *n.* zümrüt
empire *n.* imparatorluk
empty *adj.* boş
end *n.* son
enemy *n.* düşman
energy *n.* enerji
engaged (to be married) *adj.* nişanlı
engineer *n.* mühendis
England *n.* İngiltere
English *adj./n.* İngiliz; İngilizce *(language)*
(be) enough *v.* yetmek

enter *v.* girmek
entrance *n.* giriş
envelope *n.* zarf
environment *n.* çevre
era *n.* çağ
escape *v.* kaçmak
et cetera (etc.) vesaire (v.s.)
Europe *n.* Avrupa
evening *n.* akşam
event *n.* olay
every *adj.* her
everybody *pron.* herkes
example *n.* örnek; for example mesela
excavation *n.* kazı
excitement *n.* heyecan
excluded *adj.* hariç
exhibition *n.* sergi
exit *n.* çıkış
expense *n.* masraf
expensive *adj.* pahalı
experience *n.* tecrübe
experiment *n.* tecrübe
expert *n.* uzman
explain *v.* açıklamak, anlatmak
explosion *n.* patlama
export *n.* ihraç, ihracat
extra *adj./n.* ek
eye *n.* göz

F

face *n.* yüz
factory *n.* fabrika
faint *v.* bayılmak
fall *n.* sonbahar *(autumn)*; *v.* düşmek

family *n.* aile
family name *n.* soyadı
famous *adj.* meşhur, ünlü
far *adv.* uzak
farm *n.* çiftlik
fast *adj./adv.* ileri *(clock, watch)*; çabuk, hızlı
    (rapid, quick)
fast *v.* oruç tutmak
fat *adj.* şişman; *n.* yağ
father *n.* baba, ata
faucet *n.* musluk
February *n.* şubat
fee *n.* ücret
feel *v.* hissetmek
feel happy *v.* sevinmek
feeling *n.* duygu
festival *(religious)* *n.* bayram
fever *n.* ateş
few *adj./n.* az; **a few** *adj.* birkaç
fiancé(e) *n.* nişanlı
field *(agricultural)* *n.* tarla
fifty *n.* elli
fig *n.* incir
file *(dossier)* *n.* dosya
film *(camera)* *n.* film, filim
finally *adv.* nihayet
find *v.* bulmak
finger *n.* parmak
fingernail *n.* tırnak
finish *v. tr.* bitirmek
(be) finished *v. intr.* bitmek
fire *n.* ateş; yangın *(destructive fire)*
fire department *n.* itfaiye
fire extinguisher *n.* söndürücü
first *adj.* birinci, ilk
fish *n.* balık

five *n.* beş
flag *n.* bayrak
flat *adj.* düz
flood *n.* sel
floor *n.* taban
flour *n.* un
flow *v.* akmak
flower *n.* çiçek
flowerpot *n.* saksı
fly *n.* sinek *(insect)*; *v.* uçmak
fog *n.* sis
follow *v.* izlemek, takip etmek
food *n.* yemek
foot *n.* ayak
for *prep.* için
for example mesela
forbidden *adj.* yasak
forehead *n.* alın
foreign currency exchange *n.* kambiyo
foreigner *n.* yabancı
forest *n.* orman
forget *v.* unutmak
forgive *v.* affetmek
fork *n.* çatal
former *adj.* eski
fortress *n.* kale
forty *n.* kırk
forward part *n.* ileri
fountain *n.* çeşme
four *n.* dört
free *adj.* özgür; serbest; bedava *(price)*
freedom *n.* hürriyet, özgürlük
fresh *adj.* taze
Friday *n.* cuma
fried *adj.* kızartma, tava
friend *n.* arkadaş, dost

front *n.* ön; **(in) front (of)** *prep.* önünde *(-in/-ın/-ün/-un)*
fruit *n.* meyve
frying pan *n.* tava
fuel *(for heating)* *n.* yakıt
full *adj.* dolu
(have) fun *v.* eğlenmek
funeral ceremony *n.* cenaze töreni
fur *n.* kürk
(electric) fuse *n.* sigorta
future *n.* gelecek

G

game *n.* oyun
garbage *n.* çöp
garbanzo *n.* nohut
garden *n.* bahçe
garlic *n.* sarmısak
gasoline *n.* benzin
gate *n.* kapı
generally *adv.* genellikle
gentleman *n.* bay, bey
German *adj./n.* Alman; Almanca *(language)*
Germany *n.* Almanya
get *v.* almak
get off *v.* inmek *(-den/-dan)*
get on *v.* binmek *(-e/-a)*
get up *v.* kalkmak
gift *n.* hediye
girl *n.* kız
give *v.* vermek
give back *v.* iade etmek
give up *v.* vazgeçmek *(-den/-dan)*
glass *n.* bardak *(drinking)*; cam *(material)*
(eye)glasses *n.* gözlük

glue *n.* tutkal

go *v.* gitmek

go down *v.* inmek

go in(to) *v.* girmek

go out *v.* çıkmak

goat *n.* keçi

god *n.* tanrı

goddess *n.* tanrıça

God *n.* Allah

gold *n.* altın

good *adj.* iyi

Good morning! *interj.* Günaydın!

government *n.* hükümet

governor *(of a province)* *n.* vali

graduate *(from school, college, etc.)* *n.* mezun;
    v. mezun olmak

gram *n.* gram

grandchild *n.* torun

grandfather *n.* büyükbaba, dede *(no distinction between
    maternal and paternal)*

grandmother *n.* anneanne *(maternal)*; büyükanne
    (paternal)

grape *n.* üzüm

grapefruit *n.* greyfurt

gravel *n.* çakıl

grease *n.* yağ

great *adj.* büyük

Greece *n.* Yunanistan

Greek *adj./n.* Yunan *(of Greece)*, Rum *(of Cyprus,
    Turkey, etc.)*; Yunanca, Rumca *(language)*

green *adj.* yeşil

greeting *n.* selam

grilled *adj.* ızgara

grocer *n.* bakkal

ground floor *n.* zemin, zemin katı

ground meat *n.* kıyma**

guard *n.* bekçi
guess *n.* tahmin
guest *n.* misafir
guide *n.* rehber
gun *n.* silah; tabanca *(pistol)*, tüfek *(rifle)*

H

hair *n.* kıl; saç *(on a person's head)*
half *n.* buçuk *(after numerals)*; yarı; *adj.* yarım
hammer *n.* çekiç
hand *n.* el
handkerchief *n.* mendil
handle *n.* sap
happen *v.* olmak
happy *adj.* mutlu
harbor *n.* liman
hard *adj.* sert *(tough)*; zor *(difficult)*
hat *n.* şapka
have *v.* *(-in/-ın/-ün/-un)* + var *(positive)*/yok *(negative)*
⠀⠀⠀⠀[See Grammar Section Q.11]
hazelnut *n.* fındık
he *pron.* o
head *n.* kafa *(body)*; baş *(body; leader; beginning)*
headquarters *n.* merkez
health *n.* sağlık
hear *v.* duymak, işitmek
heart *n.* kalp, yürek
heating system *n.* kalorifer
heavy *adj.* ağır
hell *n.* cehennem
hello *interj.* merhaba; alo *(answering the telephone)*
help *n.* yardım; *v.* yardım etmek *(-e/-a)*
henna *n.* kına
here *adv.* burada

hide *v.* saklamak
high *adj.* yüksek
high school *n.* lise
hill *n.* tepe
history *n.* tarih
hit *v.* vurmak
hold *v.* tutmak
hole *n.* delik
holiday *n.* bayram *(religious or national)*, tatil
homeland *n.* vatan, yurt
homework *n.* ödev
honey *n.* bal
honor *n.* şeref, onur; namus *(integrity)*
hook *n.* çengel
hope *n.* umut, ümit; *v.* ummak, ümit etmek
horse *n.* at
hospital *n.* hastane
hot *adj.* sıcak *(temperature)*; acı *(spicy)*
hotel *n.* otel
hour *n.* saat
house *n.* ev
how *adv.* nasıl?
how many *adv.* kaç?
however *conj.* ancak
human being *n.* insan
hundred *n.* yüz
hungry *adj.* aç; **to feel hungry** *v.* acıkmak
hurry *n.* acele
hurt *v. intr.* ağrımak; *v. tr.* incitmek, yaralamak
husband *n.* eş, koca

I

I *pron.* ben
I wonder if...? Acaba

ice *n.* buz
ice cream *n.* dondurma
icebox *n.* buzdolabı
identity *n.* kimlik, hüviyet
identity card *n.* kimlik belgesi, kimlik kartı
if *conj.* eğer; -se/-sa
immediately *adv.* derhal, hemen
import *n.* ithal, ithalat
importance *n.* önem
important *adj.* mühim, önemli
in *prep.* -de/-da, -(y)e/-(y)a
in any case *adv.* zaten
in spite of *postp.* rağmen *(-e/-a)*
included *adj.* dahil
inconvenience *n.* zahmet
independence *n.* bağımsızlık, istiklal
information *n.* bilgi *(help desk)*; danışma
inheritance *n.* miras
insect *n.* böcek
inside *n.* içeri
instead of *prep.* yerinde *(-in/-ın/-ün/-un)*
insult *n.* hakaret
insurance *n.* sigorta
intelligent *adj.* akıllı
intensive *adj.* yoğun
interest *(banking) n.* faiz
(be) interested in *v.* ilgilenmek *(-le/-la)*
interesting *adj.* ilginç
interior *n.* iç
interpreter *n.* tercüman
interval *n.* ara
investment *n.* yatırım
invite *v.* davet etmek
iron *n.* demir *(metal)*; ütü *(for ironing clothes)*
island *n.* ada
it *pron.* o

J

(sports) jacket *n.* ceket
jam *n.* reçel
January *n.* ocak
Jew/Jewish *adj./n.* Musevi, Yahudi
joke *n.* şaka
journey *n.* seyahat
joy *n.* neşe, sevinç
Judaism *n.* Musevilik
July *n.* temmuz
June *n.* haziran
just about to *prep.* üzere

K

key *n.* ahahtar
kill *v.* öldürmek
kilogram *n.* kilo
kilometer *n.* kilometre
kind *adj.* iyi kalpli; *n.* çeşit *(type)*
king *n.* kral
kiss *v.* öpmek
kitchen *n.* mutfak
knee *n.* diz
knife *n.* bıçak
know *v.* bilmek
Kurd *adj./n.* Kürt

L

lacking *adj.* eksik
ladder *n.* merdiven
lady *n.* hanım, hanımefendi

lake *n.* göl
lamb *n.* kuzu
lamp *n.* lamba
language *n.* dil
last *adj.* geçen *(past time)*; son *(final)*
late *adj.* geç
laugh *v.* gülmek
laundry *n.* çamaşır
lavatory *n.* tuvalet
law *n.* kanun *(regulation)*; hukuk *(jurisprudence)*
lawyer *n.* avukat
layer *n.* tabaka
lazy *adj.* tembel
lead *(metal) n.* kurşun
leaf *n.* yaprak
learn *v.* öğrenmek
leather *n.* deri
leave *v.* bırakmak; ayrılmak *(-den/-dan)*
leave (of absence) *n.* izin
lecture *n.* konferans, konuşma
left (side) *adj./n.* sol
leg *n.* bacak
legend *n.* efsane
lemon *n.* limon
lentil *n.* mercimek
lesson *n.* ders
letter *n.* mektup
lettuce *n.* salata
library *n.* kütüphane
license plate *n.* plaka
lie *(falsehood) n.* yalan
life *n.* hayat, ömür
lift up *v.* kaldırmak
light *adj.* açık *(color)*; hafif *(weight; food, sleep, etc.)*;
    n. ışık
lightning flash *n.* şimşek, yıldırım

like *prep.* gibi; *v.* beğenmek, sevmek
linden tea *n.* ıhlamur
line *n.* çizgi; sıra *(organized waiting)*
linen *n.* keten
lip *n.* dudak
liquid *n.* sıvı
listen to *v.* dinlemek *(-i/-ı/-ü/-u)*
literature *n.* edebiyat
little *adj.* az *(amount)*; küçük *(size, age)*; **a little** *adj.* biraz
live *v.* oturmak, yaşamak
lively *adj.* canlı
liver *n.* ciğer
living room *n.* salon
loan *n.* ödünç; *v.* ödünç vermek
long *adj.* uzun
look at *v.* bakmak *(-e/-a)*
look for *v.* aramak *(-i/-ı)*
Look out! Dikkat!
loose *adj.* gevşek
loose-fitting *adj.* bol
lose *v.* kaybetmek
(be) lost *v.* kaybolmak
lottery *n.* piyango
love *v.* sevmek
low *adj.* alçak *(vile)*; alt, aşağı *(below)*
luck *n.* şans; **Good luck!** İyi şanslar!
lung(s) *n.* akciğer

M

machine *n.* makina
magazine *n.* dergi
mail *n.* posta
make *v.* yapmak
man *n.* adam, erkek

management *n.* idare, yönetim
manager *n.* yönetmen, yönetici
many *adj.* çok
map *n.* harita
marbled *(paper) adj.* ebru
March *n.* mart
market *n.* pazar, market
married *adj.* evli
master workman *n.* usta
match *(for fire) n.* kibrit
May *n.* mayıs
maybe *adv.* belki
meaning *n.* mana
measure *v.* ölçmek
meat *n.* et
medical treatment *n.* tedavi
medicine *n.* ilaç
Mediterranean Sea *n.* Akdeniz
meet *v.* buluşmak *(come together)*; karşılamak *(-i/-ı/-ü/-u)*
    (to go to meet); tanışmak *(-le/-la) (make the*
    acquaintance of)
meeting *n.* toplantı
melon *n.* kavun
member *(of a group) n.* üye
metal *n.* maden
meter *n.* metre
meticulous *adj.* titiz
middle *adj./n.* orta
migrant *n.* göçmen
milk *n.* süt
million *n.* milyon
minaret *n.* minare
mine *(for metals) n.* maden
mineral *n.* maden
minister *(government) n.* bakan
ministry *(government) n.* bakanlık

mint, peppermint *n.* nane
minute *(time) n.* dakika `
mirror *n.* ayna
mistake *n.* yanlış
mixed *adj.* karışık
molestation *n.* tecavüz
moment *n.* an
Monday *n.* pazartesi
money *n.* para
month *n.* ay
moon *n.* ay
more *adj./adv.* daha
morning *n.* sabah
mosque *n.* cami
mosquito *n.* sivrisinek
most *adj.* en
mother *n.* ana, anne
motion *n.* hareket
mountain *n.* dağ
mouse *n.* fare
moustache *n.* bıyık
mouth *n.* ağız
move *v.* hareket etmek; taşınmak *(to a new residence or
    place of business)*
movie *n.* sinema
movie theater *n.* sinema
Mr. *n.* bay *(followed by the surname)*, bey *(placed after
    the first name)*
Mrs./Ms./Miss *n.* bayan *(followed by the surname)*,
    hanım *(placed after the first name)*
much *adj./adv.* çok
mud *n.* çamur
municipality *n.* belediye
muscle *n.* kas
museum *n.* müze
mushroom *n.* mantar

music *n.* müzik
Muslim *adj./n.* Müslüman
mussel *n.* midye
mustard *n.* hardal

N

nail *(metal)* *n.* çivi
naked *adj.* çıplak
name *n.* ad, isim
napkin *n.* peçete
narrow *adj.* dar
nation *n.* millet, ulus
national *adj.* milli
native country *(fatherland, motherland)* *n.* vatan
natural sciences *n.* fen
nature *n.* doğa
near *adj./adv.* yakın
(to be) necessary *v.* gerekmek, lazım
necessity *n.* ihtiyaç
neck *n.* boyun
neighbor *n.* komşu
neighborhood *n.* mahalle
nephew *n.* yeğen
new *adj.* yeni
news *n.* haber
newspaper *n.* gazete
next *adj.* ertesi *(day, week, year)*; gelecek, sonraki
niece *n.* yeğen
night *n.* gece
nightingale *n.* bülbül
nine *n.* dokuz
ninety *n.* doksan
no *adv.* hayır
no one *pron.* kimse *(used with a negative verb)*

noise *n.* gürültü
noon *n.* öğle
normal *adj.* normal
north *n.* kuzey
nose *n.* burun
not *adv.* değil
notebook *n.* defter
nothing *n.* hiç
November *n.* kasım
now *adv.* şimdi
number *n.* numara

O

oat *n.* yulaf
obligation *n.* borç, mecburiyet
October *n.* ekim
of *prep.* -in/-ın/-ün/-un
of course tabii
office *n.* büro, ofis
official *adj.* resmi
often *adv.* çok defa
oh *interj.* ya; öğle mi? *(is that so?)*
oil *n.* yağ
okay *adv.* peki, tamam
old *adj.* eski *(thing)*; ihtiyar, yaşlı *(person)*
olive *n.* zeytin; olive oil *n.* zeytin yağı
(person) on duty *n.* nöbetçi
one *n.* bir
onion *n.* soğan
only *adv.* yalnız
open *adj.* açık; *v.* açmak
opportunity *n.* fırsat
opposite *adj./prep.* karşı, ters

or *conj.* veya, yahut, yoksa
orange *(fruit) n.* portakal
order *(something) v.* ısmarlamak
other *adj.* başka; diğer; öbür
Ottoman *adj./n.* Osmanlı
out *adj./adv.* dışarı
out of order *adj.* arızalı
outside *n.* dış, dışarı
oven *n.* fırın
overcoat *n.* palto
own *adj.* kendi; *v.* sahip olmak *(-e/-a)*
owner *n.* sahip

P

package *n.* paket
page *(book, newspaper, etc.) n.* sayfa
pain *n.* ağrı, acı
paint *n.* boya
painter *n.* ressam
painting *n.* resim
palace *n.* saray
pants *n.* pantolon
paper *n.* kâğıt
paradise *n.* cennet
pardon *v.* affetmek; **Pardon me!** Affedersiniz!
park *n.* park; *v.* park etmek *(a vehicle)*
parking lot *n.* park yeri, otopark
parliament *n.* meclis, parlamento
parsley *n.* maydanoz
part *n.* kısım
pass *v.* geçmek
passenger *n.* yolcu
passport *n.* pasaport

pastry shop *n.* pastane
pay *v.* ödemek
pea(s) *n.* bezelye
peace *n.* barış; huzur *(peace of mind)*
peanut *n.* fıstık
pear *n.* armut
pearl *n.* inci
pedestrian *n.* yaya
pen *n.* kalem
penalty *n.* ceza
pencil *n.* kalem, kurşunkalem
pepper *n.* biber
percent *n.* yüzde
permission *n.* izin, müsaade
person *n.* insan, kişi
pharmacy *n.* eczane
photograph *n.* fotoğraf
phyllo *(thin sheet of dough)* *n.* yufka
pickle *n.* turşu
picture *n.* resim
piece *n.* parça
pig *n.* domuz
pilgrimage *n.* hac
pillow *n.* yastık
pine tree *n.* çam
pink *adj./n.* pembe
pipe *n.* boru; pipo *(tobacco)*
pistachio *n.* fıstık, şamfıstığı
pistol *n.* tabanca
pit *n.* çukur; çekirdek *(fruit)*
pity *n.* yazık
place *n.* yer
plain *adj.* sade; *n.* ova
plan *n.* plan; *v.* planlamak
plate *n.* tabak

plateau *(geog.)* *n.* yayla
play *n.* oyun; *v.* oynamak; çalmak *(a musical instrument)*
playing field *n.* saha
pleasant *adj.* hoş
please *adv.* lütfen
pleased *adj.* memnun
pleasure *n.* keyif, zevk
plentiful *adj.* bol
plug *(on an electrical cord)* *n.* fiş
plum *n.* erik
pocket *n.* cep
poem *n.* şiir
poet *n.* şair
point *(dot or place)* *n.* nokta
point of view *n.* bakım
poison *n.* zehir
police *n.* polis
police station *n.* karakol
polite *adj.* nazik, terbiyeli
poor *adj.* fakir *(no money)*; zavallı *(miserable, pitiful)*
poplar tree *n.* kavak
populace *n.* halk
population *n.* nüfus
pork *n.* domuz eti
port *(harbor)* *n.* liman
possibility *n.* imkân
possible *adj.* mümkün
post office *n.* postane, PTT
potato *n.* patates
pour *v.* dökmek
powder *n.* toz, pudra
power *n.* güç
preference *n.* tercih
pregnant *adj.* hamile
president *n.* başkan; cumhurbaşkanı *(of the republic)*

press *n.* yayınevi *(publishing house)*; *v.* basmak
pretty *adj.* güzel
price *n.* fiyat
price increase *n.* zam
pride *n.* gurur
priest *n.* papaz
prime minister *n.* başbakan
prison *n.* hapishane
private *adj.* özel
probability *n.* ihtimal
probably *adv.* galiba
problem *n.* problem, sorun
production *n.* üretim
profession *n.* meslek
professor *n.* profesör
prohibited *adj.* yasak
promise *n.* söz; *v.* söz vermek *(-e/-a)*
property *n.* mal
protect *v.* korumak
publication *n.* yayın, yayım
pull *v.* çekmek
pumpkin *n.* balkabağı
push *v.* itmek
put *v.* koymak

Q

quantity *n.* miktar
quarrel *n.* kavga
quarter *(one fourth)* *n.* çeyrek
queen *n.* kraliçe
question *n.* soru
quilt *n.* yorgan
quince *n.* ayva
quit *v.* bırakmak

R

rabbit *n.* tavşan
radio *n.* radyo
rain *n.* yağmur; *v.* yağmur yağmak
rape *n.* tecavüz
razor *n.* tıraş makinası
read *v.* okumak
ready *adj.* hazır
real estate *n.* emlak
really *adv.* gerçekten, hakikaten
recognize *v.* tanımak
recommendation *n.* tavsiye
red *adj./n.* kırmızı
reduction *(in price) n.* indirim
refrigerator *n.* buzdolabı
refuse *v.* reddetmek
region *n.* bölge
registered *(letter) adj.* taahhütlü
registration *n.* kayıt
relative *(family) n.* akraba
religion *n.* din
remain *v.* kalmak
remedy *n.* çare
remember *v.* hatırlamak
remove *v.* çıkarmak, kaldırmak
rent *(money)*, **renting** *n.* kira
repeat *v.* tekrarlamak
representative *(agent) n.* temsilci
republic *n.* cumhuriyet
request *v.* rica etmek
resemble *v.* benzemek *(-e/-a)*
reserve, set aside *v.* ayırtmak
residence permit *n.* ikamet tezkeresi
resignation *(from a position) n.* istifa
rest *v.* dinlenmek

rest break *n.* mola

restaurant *n.* lokanta, restoran

retired *(worker, etc.) adj./n.* emekli

return *v.* dönmek

reverse *n.* ters

rice *n.* pirinç *(uncooked grains)*; pilav *(cooked)*

rich *adj.* zengin

ride *v.* binmek *(-e/-a)*

rifle *n.* tüfek

right *adj.* haklı *(correct)*; *n.* hak

right *(side) adj./n.* sağ

ring *n.* yüzük *(worn on a finger)*; *v.* çalmak *(ring a doorbell)*

rise *v.* yükselmek

river *n.* nehir

road *n.* yol

romaine lettuce *n.* marul

room *n.* oda

rope *n.* ip, halat

rose *n.* gül

rotten *adj.* çürük

round *adj.* yuvarlak

row *n.* sıra

rubber *(material) n.* lastik

rug *n.* halı

ruins *n.* harabe

rule *(regulation) n.* kural

run *v.* koşmak

run away *v.* kaçmak

rust *v.* paslanmak

S

sacrifice *n.* kurban; fedakârlık *(self-sacrifice, self-denial)*

safety *n.* emniyet, güvenlik

salad *n.* salata
salary *n.* maaş
salesman/woman *n.* satıcı
salt *n.* tuz
salty *adj.* tuzlu
same *adj./n.* aynı
sand *n.* kum
sarcophagus *n.* lahit
Saturday *n.* cumartesi
sausage *n.* sosis, sucuk
save *(rescue)* *v.* kurtarmak
say *v.* demek, söylemek
scandal *n.* rezalet
school *n.* okul
scissors *n.* makas
scorpion *n.* akrep
screw *n.* vida
screwdriver *n.* tornavida
sculptor *n.* heykeltıraş
sculpture *n.* heykel, heykeltıraşlık
sea *n.* deniz
season *n.* mevsim
seat *n.* sandalye, yer
secret *adj.* gizli
secretary *n.* sekreter
see *v.* görmek
seek *v.* aramak
seldom *adv.* az
self *n.* kendi
sell *v.* satmak
send *v.* göndermek, yollamak
sensitive *adj.* hassas
sentence *(grammar)* *n.* cümle
separate *adj.* ayrı; *v.* ayırmak
September *n.* eylül
serious *adj.* ağır, ciddi

set up *v.* kurmak
seven *n.* yedi
seventy *n.* yetmiş
shade *n.* gölge
shadow *n.* gölge
shameful behavior *n.* ayıp
shape *n.* şekil
share *v.* paylaşmak
shave *n.* tıraş
she *pron.* o
sheep *n.* koyun
(bed)sheet *n.* çarşaf
shelf *n.* raf
shell *n.* kabuk
shepherd *n.* çoban
shine *v.* parlamak
ship *n.* gemi
shirt *n.* gömlek
shoe *n.* ayakkabı
shop *n.* dükkân, mağaza; *v.* alışveriş etmek
shopping *n.* alışveriş
shore *n.* sahil
short *adj.* kısa
shoulder *n.* omuz
shovel *n.* kürek
show *n.* temsil *(performance)*; sergi *(exhibition)*;
    v. göstermek
shower *n.* duş
sick *adj.* hasta
side *n.* taraf, yan
sidewalk *n.* kaldırım
sign *v.* imzalamak
signature *n.* imza
(be) silent *v.* susmak
silk *n.* ipek
silver *adj./n.* gümüş

sin *n.* günah

since *prep.* beri (*-den/-dan*)

sing *v.* söylemek

single *adj.* tek

sir *n.* beyefendi

sister *n.* kızkardeş

sister-in-law *n.* yenge

sit *v.* oturmak

situation *n.* durum

six *n.* altı

sixty *n.* altmış

size *n.* boy, büyüklük

ski *n.* kayak

skin *n.* deri

skirt *n.* etek

sky *n.* gök

sleep *n.* uyku; *v.* uyumak

slender *adj.* ince

slice *n.* dilim

slipper *n.* terlik

slippery *adj.* kaygan

slow *adj.* yavaş

slowly *adv.* yavaş yavaş

small *adj.* küçük

smell *n.* koku; *v.* kokmak

smoke *n.* duman; *v.* içmek (*cigarette*)

snow *n.* kar; *v.* kar yağmak

soap *n.* sabun

sock (*clothing*) *n.* çorap

soft *adj.* yumuşak

soldier *n.* asker

sole *n.* taban (*foot, shoe*); dilbalığı (*fish*)

some *adj.* bazı

someone *pron.* kimse

sometimes *adv.* bazen, bazan

son *n.* oğul

song *n.* şarkı
soul *n.* can, ruh
sound *n.* ses
soup *n.* çorba
sour *adj.* ekşi
source *n.* kaynak
south *n.* güney
space *(place) n.* alan
spare *n.* yedek
speak *v.* konuşmak
speak about *v.* bahsetmek *(-den/-dan)*
special *adj.* özel
speed *n.* hız
spider *n.* örümcek
spinach *n.* ıspanak
spit *(skewer) n.* şiş
spoil *v.* bozmak
sponge *n.* sünger
spoon *n.* kaşık
sport(s) *n.* spor
spot *(stain) n.* leke
spring *n.* bahar, ilkbahar *(season)*; pınar *(water)*
(public) square *n.* meydan
squid *n.* kalamar
stairs *n.* merdiven
(postage) stamp *n.* pul
stand up *v.* kalkmak
star *n.* yıldız
state *n.* durum, hal *(condition)*; devlet *(political unit)*
station *n.* istasyonu
statue *n.* heykel
steal *v.* çalmak
steamship *n.* vapur
steel *n.* çelik
step on *v.* basmak
stick *v. intr.* yapışmak

still *adv.* hâlâ, henüz
stomach *n.* mide, karın
stone *n.* taş
stop *n.* durak *(bus, train)*; *v.* durmak
stop by briefly *v.* uğramak *(-e/-a)*
stopped up *adj.* tıkalı
stork *n.* leylek
storm *n.* fırtına
story *n.* hikâye, öykü; kat *(building)*
stove *n.* ocak
straight *adj./adv.* doğru
strainer *n.* süzgeç
strait *n.* boğaz
strange *adj.* garip, tuhaf
strawberry *n.* çilek
street *n.* cadde, sokak
strength *n.* güç, kuvvet
string *n.* ip
stroll *v.* dolaşmak
student *n.* öğrenci
study *v.* okumak
stupid *adj.* aptal
subject *(topic)* *n.* konu
subscription *n.* abone
succeed in *v.* başarmak *(-i/-ı)*
suddenly *adv.* birdenbire
sugar *n.* şeker
suitable *adj.* uygun *(-e/-a)*
suitcase *n.* valiz, bagaj
summary *n.* özet
summer *n.* yaz
sun *n.* güneş
(be) sunburned *v.* yanmak
Sunday *n.* pazar
(get) suntanned *v.* yanmak
support *v.* desteklemek

sure (of) *adj.* emin *(-den/-dan)*
surely *adv.* herhalde
surname *n.* soyadı
(be) surprised *v.* şaşırmak
suspicion *n.* şüphe
sweat *n.* ter
sweet *adj.* tatlı
swim *v.* yüzmek
sword *n.* kılıç
Syria *n.* Suriye

T

table *n.* masa
tail *n.* kuyruk
tailor *n.* terzi
take *v.* almak; sürmek *(a certain amount of time)*
take (a photograph) *v.* (fotoğraf) çekmek
talk (with) *v.* görüşmek *(-le/-la)*
tall *(person) adj.* uzun boylu
target *n.* hedef
tasty *adj.* lezzetli
tax *n.* vergi
taxi *n.* taksi
tea *n.* çay
teach *v.* öğretmek
teacher *n.* hoca, öğretmen
tear *n.* gözyaşı, yaş *(in the eyes)*; *v.* yırtmak *(rip)*
telephone *n.* telefon; *v.* telefon etmek *(-e/-a)*
telephone directory *n.* telefon rehberi
television *n.* televizyon
tell *v.* söylemek
ten *n.* on
tent *n.* çadır
test *(exam) n.* sınav

Thank you Teşekkür ederim, mersi

that *adj./pron.* şu, o

theater *n.* tiyatro

there *adv.* orada; oraya *(to that place)*; oradan *(from that place)*

there is/are *v.* var

there is/are not *v.* yok

thick *adj.* kalın

thief *n.* hırsız

thing *n.* şey

think *v.* sanmak

think (about) *v.* düşünmek *(-i/-ı/-ü/-u)*

(be) thirsty *v.* susamak

thirty *n.* otuz

this *adj./pron.* bu, şu

thought *n.* fikir

thousand *n.* bin

three *n.* üç

throat *n.* boğaz

throw, throw away *v.* atmak

Thursday *n.* perşembe

ticket *n.* bilet

ticket window *n.* gişe

time *n.* vakit, zaman; defa, kere *(as in "two times")*

time of day *n.* saat

tiny *adj.* ufak

tire *(automobile)* *n.* lastik

(be, get) tired *v.* yorulmak

tired *adj.* yorgun

today *adv.* bugün

toe *n.* parmak, ayak parmağı

together *adv.* beraber

toilet *n.* tuvalet

tomato *n.* domates

tomb *n.* mezar

tomorrow *n.* yarın

tongue *n.* dil
too (much/many) *adv.* fazla
(be) too lazy to (do something) *v.* üşenmek *(-e/-a)*
tooth *n.* diş
toothbrush *n.* diş fırçası
toothpaste *n.* diş macunu
top *n.* üst
touch *v.* dokunmak *(-e/-a)*
tour *n.* gezi, tur; *v.* gezmek
tourism *n.* turizm
tourist *n.* turist
towel *n.* havlu
tower *n.* kule
town *n.* şehir; kasaba *(small town)*
traffic *(cars)* *n.* trafik
traffic circle *n.* göbek
train *n.* tren
train station *n.* gar
translate *v.* çevirmek, tercüme etmek
translation *n.* tercüme
transport *n.* nakliyat
trap *n.* tuzak
traveler *n.* yolcu
tray *n.* tepsi
treasure *n.* define, hazine
tree *n.* ağaç
trip *(journey)* *n.* sefer, seyahat, yolculuk
trouble *n.* sıkıntı; zahmet *(inconvenience)*
true *adj.* doğru, gerçek
try *v.* denemek
tube *n.* tüp; iç lastik *(car tire)*
Tuesday *n.* salı
tuna *n.* palamut, tonbalığı
Turk *n.* Türk
turkey *(bird)* *n.* hindi
Turkey *n.* Türkiye

Turkish *adj.* Türk
Turkish bath *n.* hamam
Turkish delight *n.* lokum
Turkish language *n.* Türkçe
turn *n.* sıra *(as in "it's my turn")*; *v.* dönmek *(rotate)*
turn on *v.* açmak
turn to *v.* sapmak
twenty *n.* yirmi
two *n.* iki

U

ugly *adj.* çirkin
umbrella *n.* şemsiye
uncle *n.* dayı *(maternal)*; amca *(paternal)*
uncomfortable *adj.* rahatsız
underground *adj.* yeraltı
underside *n.* alt
understand *v.* anlamak
unfortunately *adv.* maalesef
united *adj.* birleşik
university *n.* üniversite
unmarried *adj.* bekâr
until *prep.* kadar *(-e/-a)*
unwell *adj.* rahatsız
upkeep *n.* bakım
upper part *n.* yukarı
upper surface *n.* üst, üzeri
(be) upset *v.* üzülmek *(-e/-a)*
USA (United States of America) *n.* ABD (Amerika
    Birleşik Devletleri)
use *v.* kullanmak
useful *adj.* faydalı, yararlı
usefulness *n.* fayda

V

vacation *n.* tatil
vegetable *n.* sebze
very *adv.* çok
victory *n.* zafer
view *n.* manzara
vile *adj.* alçak
village *n.* köy
villager *n.* köylü
vinegar *n.* sirke
violin *n.* keman
visit *n.* ziyaret; *v.* ziyaret etmek
voice *n.* ses

W

wage increase *n.* zam
wait for *v.* beklemek *(-i/-ı)*
waiter *n.* garson
wake up *v. intr.* uyanmak
walk *n.* yürüyüş; *v.* yürümek
wall *n.* duvar
wallet *n.* cüzdan
walnut *n.* ceviz
want *v.* istemek
war *n.* savaş
warm up *v.* ısınmak
wash *v.* yıkamak
washroom *n.* lavabo
watch *v.* seyretmek
(wrist)watch *n.* saat
watchman *n.* bekçi
water *n.* su
watermelon *n.* karpuz

wave *(water; heat or cold) n.* dalga

(in this/that) way *adv.* şöyle

wax *n.* mum

we *pron.* biz

weak *adj.* zayıf

weapon *n.* silah

wear *v.* giymek

weather *n.* hava

wedding *n.* düğün, nikâh

Wednesday *n.* çarşamba

week *n.* hafta

weigh *v.* tartmak

weight *n.* ağırlık

well *adj./adv.* iyi; *n.* kuyu

west *n.* batı

wet *adj.* ıslak

wharf *n.* iskele

what *pron.* ne?

wheel *n.* tekerlek

where *adv.* nerede?; nereye? *(to where?)*; nereden?
　　　(from where?)

which *adj./pron.* hangi?

white *adj./n.* beyaz, ak

who *pron.* kim?

whole *adj.* bütün, tam; *n.* tamam

why *adv.* neden? niçin? niye?

wide *adj.* geniş

widespread *adj.* yaygın

wife *n.* eş, karı

win *v.* kazanmak

wind *n.* rüzgâr

window *n.* pencere

wine *n.* şarap

wing *n.* kanat

winter *n.* kış

wipe *v.* silmek

wire *n.* tel
wish *n.* istek; *v.* dilemek, istemek
with *prep.* ile
woman *n.* kadın
wonderful *adj.* harika
wood *n.* ahşap, odun, tahta
wool *n.* yün
word *n.* kelime, söz
work *n.* iş; *v.* çalışmak
work (of art) *n.* eser
worker *n.* işçi
world *n.* dünya
worth *n.* değer
wound *n.* yara
wrist *n.* bilek
write *v.* yazmak
writer *n.* yazar
writing *n.* yazı

Y

year *n.* sene, yıl
yellow *adj.* sarı
yes *adv.* evet
Yes, sir/madam! *(as reply) interj.* Efendim!
yesterday *n.* dün
yet *(in negative sentences) adv.* henüz
yogurt *n.* yoğurt
you *pron.* sen *(sing. informal)*, siz *(sing. formal; and pl.)*
young *adj./n.* genç

Z

zero *n.* sıfır
zucchini *n.* kabak

TURKISH PHRASEBOOK

BASIC EXPRESSIONS

Basic Expressions

Yes.
Evet.

No.
Hayır.

Please.
Lütfen.

Good morning.
Günaydın.

Hello, hi.
Merhaba. *(informal)*

Hello, good-bye.
İyi günler.
(Said during the daytime; appropriate to say both when entering and leaving a shop or office.)

Welcome!
Hoş geldiniz! (Said by the person who welcomes the guest.)
Hoş bulduk! (Said by the arriving guest.)
[This two-part formula is absolutely standard.]

Good evening.
İyi akşamlar.
(Said during the evening; appropriate to say both upon meeting and upon leaving.)

Good night.
İyi geceler.
(Used when about to retire for the night.)

Good-bye.

Allaha ısmarladık. [Pronounced: Alas-**mal**-dık] (Said by the person leaving.)

Güle güle. (Said by the person staying.)

[Another absolutely standard two-part formula.]

Good-bye.

Hoşça kalın.

(Modern, without religious overtones; used by TV announcers, for example.)

Thank you.

Teşekkür ederim.

(Do not be intimidated by this long phrase! Break it down into syllables: te-şek-kür e-der-im, making sure to double the "k" sound, with the accent on "kür.")

Thank you.

Mersi.

(This French borrowing can also be used.)

You're welcome.

Bir şey değil. (*lit.* It is nothing.) / **Rica ederim.**

How are you?

Nasılsınız? (Accent on the first syllable.)

I am fine, thank you. How are you?

İyiyim, teşekkür ederim. Siz nasılsınız?

(Using the pronoun **siz** emphasizes "you": and <u>you</u>, how are you?)

Excuse me.

Affedersiniz.

I beg your pardon; I apologize.

Özür dilerim.

BASIC EXPRESSIONS

OK.
Tamam.

It's not important. It doesn't matter.
Önemli değil.

May it be past!
Geçmiş olsun!
(Said to someone suffering from illness or bad luck, or enduring any sort of hardship.)

Please come in! Please sit down! Please have some!
Buyurun.

I hope you enjoy the meal. Bon appétit.
Afiyet olsun. (*lit.* Let there be health.)
(<u>Note</u>: Can be said before, during, and after a meal.)

Excellent!
Elinize sağlık. / Ellerinize sağlık. (*lit.* Health to your hand(s).)
(<u>Note</u>: A standard compliment to someone who has pre-pared food.)

Common Signs; Emergencies, and When Things Don't Work

COMMON SIGNS

Entrance.
Giriş.

Exit.
Çıkış.

No entry.
Girilmez.

No smoking.
Sigara içilmez.

Danger.
Tehlike.

Stop!
Dur!

EMERGENCIES

FOR EMERGENCIES

Help!
İmdat!

Police!
Polis!

Where is/are the police?
Polis nerede?

Stop!
Dur!

Go away!
Git!

Leave me alone!
Bırak beni!

Get lost!
Defol!

Scram!
Toz ol! (*lit.* Turn to dust!)

Look out!
Dikkat!

Come here.
Gel buraya. (*informal*)

Would you please come here?
Gelir misiniz? (*polite; formal*)

Can you help me?
Yardım eder misiniz?

What happened? What's wrong?
Ne oldu?

My money has been stolen.
Param çalındı. / Paramı çaldırdım.

I have lost my passport and my wallet.
Pasaportumu ve cüzdanımı kaybettim.

I am sick.
Hastayım.

I need a doctor.
Doktor lazım.

Hospital
Hastane

I want to go to a hospital.
Hastaneye gitmek istiyorum.

Emergency room (hospital)
Acil servis

Pharmacy, drugstore
Eczane

Pharmacy open at night or during a holiday
Nöbetçi eczane
(Note: Pharmacies rotate this service.)

Toilet
Tuvalet

Fast
Çabuk

EMERGENCIES

Urgent
Acele

Slow
Yavaş

Here
Burada

There; over there
Şurada; orada

Fire
Yangın

Explosion
Patlama

WHEN THINGS DON'T WORK

It doesn't work.
Çalışmıyor.

Broken
Bozuk

Plugged up, clogged
Tıkalı

It needs to be repaired.
Tamir edilmesi lazım.

Where can I find a repairman?
Tamirci nerede bulabilirim?

DIRECTIONS

Directions

Left
Sol

Right
Sağ

Straight
Doğru / Düz / Direkt

Go straight.
Doğru gidin.

Go back.
Geri gidin.

Stop here.
Burada durun.

I'm lost.
Kayboldum.

Where?
Nerede? (*Location only; no motion is indicated*)

Where am I?
Neredeyim?

Where is the post office?
PTT nerede? / Postane nerede?
(**PTT** = *abbr.* for **Posta, Telgraf, Telefon İşletmesi**,
Post, Telegraph, and Telephone Office.)

Where is the road to Konya?
Konya yolu nerede?

Do you know where Arjantin Avenue is?
Arjantin Caddesi nerede biliyor musunuz?

To where?
Nereye? (*motion to/toward is indicated*)

Where are you going?
Nereye gidiyorsunuz?

Where do you want to go?
Nereye gitmek istiyorsunuz?

I want to go to the bus station.
Otogara gitmek istiyorum.

We want to go to this address.
Bu adrese gitmek istiyoruz.

From where?
Nereden? (*motion from is indicated*)

Where has this bus come from?
Bu otobüs nereden geldi?

Is it near?
Yakın mı?

It is near.
Yakın.

Is it far?
Uzak mı?

It is very far.
Çok uzak.

DIRECTIONS

Down
Aşağı

The city center is down the hill.
Şehir merkezi tepenin aşağısında.

Up
Yukarı

Inside; indoors
İçeride

Outside; outdoors
Dışarıda

Back; the space behind
Arka

The restaurant is behind the hotel.
Lokanta otelin arkasında.

Front; front part
Ön

The taxis are in front of the museum.
Taksiler müzenin önünde.

Side
Yan

The pastry shop is next to/beside the Park Hotel.
Pastane Park Otelinin yanında.

Ground floor (abbreviation used in elevators)
Z (= **zemin katı**)

Numbers

Zero
Sıfır

Quarter
Çeyrek

Half *(adjective)*
Yarım

A half kilo of cherries, please.
Yarım kilo kiraz, lütfen.

Half *(noun)*; half of the
Yarı

On Sunday half the grocery stores are open.
Pazar günü bakkalların yarısı açık.

One
Bir

And a half.
Buçuk.

One and a half.
Bir buçuk.

Two
İki

Three
Üç

NUMBERS

Four
Dört

Five
Beş

Six
Altı

Seven
Yedi

Eight
Sekiz

Nine
Dokuz

Ten
On

Eleven; twelve; thirteen; fourteen; *etc.*
Onbir; oniki; onüç; ondört; *etc.*

Twenty
Yirmi

Twenty-one; twenty-two; twenty-three; *etc.*
Yirmibir; yirmiiki; yirmiüç; *etc.*

Thirty
Otuz

Forty
Kırk

Fifty
Elli

Sixty
Altmış

Seventy
Yetmiş

Eighty
Seksen

Ninety
Doksan

Hundred
Yüz

Two hundred
İkiyüz

Two hundred thirty-five
İkiyüzotuzbeş *(Compound numbers are written as one word.)*

Thousand
Bin

Million
Milyon

10,500,000 TL (Turkish liras)
Onmilyonbeşyüzbin TL (Türk lirası)

Billion
Milyar

NUMBERS

First
Birinci / İlk

Second
İkinci

Third
Üçüncü

Fourth
Dördüncü

Fifth
Beşinci

One each. / One apiece.
Birer.

Two each.
İkişer.

Three each.
Üçer.

Four each.
Dörder.

Five each.
Beşer.

Health Matters

Doctor
Doktor

Nurse
Hemşire

Dentist
Dişçi

Hospital
Hastane

Doctor's office, consulting room
Muayenehane

How are you?
Nasılsınız?

I am fine.
İyiyim.

I am not well.
Rahatsızım.

I am sick.
Hastayım.

I have a cold.
Nezleyim.

I have a fever.
Ateşim var.

My head aches.
Başım ağrıyor.

… aches.
… ağrıyor.

My stomach.
Midem.

My eyes.
Gözlerim.

A tooth.
Diş.

My back.
Sırtım.

My throat.
Boğazım.

My ear.
Kulağım.

My feet.
Ayaklarım.

My knees.
Dizlerim.

What happened?
Ne oldu?

I don't know what happened.
Ne olduğunu bilmiyorum.

What is wrong with you?
Neyiniz var? / Rahatsızlığınız nedir?

What is your complaint?
Şikayetiniz ne?

I have an allergy.
Alerjim var.

He/she has an allergy.
Alerjisi var.

I am allergic to eggs.
Yumurtaya alerjim var. / Yumurtaya karşı alerjim var.

I am allergic to ...
... -e/-a alerjim var.

... dust.
Toz ...

... bee stings.
Arı sokması ...

... dairy products.
Süt ürünleri ...

A bee has stung me.
Beni arı soktu.

My glasses are broken. Where can I get them repaired?
Gözlüklerim kırıldı. Onları nerede tamir ettirebilirim?

I have high blood pressure.
Yüksek tansiyonum var.

HEALTH MATTERS

My wife is pregnant.
Eşim hamile.

I have injured my arm.
Kolumu yaraladım.

My head is spinning; I feel dizzy.
Başım dönüyor.

I have to give you a shot (injection).
Size iğne yapmam lazım. / Size iğne yapmam gerekiyor.

I do not want a shot (injection).
İğne olmak istemiyorum.

Sit down.
Oturun.

Won't you please sit down?
Oturmaz mısınız?

Lie down.
Yatın.

Take off ...
... çıkartın.

Take off your jacket.
Ceketinizi çıkartın.

Your shirt.
Gömleğinizi.

Your shoes.
Ayakkabılarınızı.

Put this on.
Bunu giyin.

Put on these slippers.
Terlikleri giyin.

Would you please wait here?
Burada bekler misiniz?

AT THE PHARMACY/DRUGSTORE

Pharmacy / Drugstore
Eczane

I want / I would like …
… istiyorum.

I want/would like to buy …
… almak istiyorum.

Medicine
İlaç

Pill
Hap

Aspirin
Aspirin

Antiseptic; disinfectant
Antiseptik ilaç

Bandage (small)
Yara bandı

Bandage (large)
Bandaj / Sargı

Shampoo
Şampuan

Comb
Tarak

Nail file
Tırnak törpüsü

Talcum powder
Talk pudrası

Lotion
Losyon

Depilatory wax
Ağda

Sanitary napkins / Tampons
Kadın bağı / Tampon
(Also referred to by brand names, such as **"Orkid"**)

Condoms
Prezervatif

How often should I take this medicine?
Bu ilacı kaç kere almam gerekiyor?

Once a day.
Günde bir kere. / Günde bir kez.

Take one pill three times a day.
Günde üç kere (üç kez) bir tane hap alın.

One tablespoonful.
Bir çorba kaşığı.

One teaspoonful.
Bir tatlı kaşığı.
(*lit.* one dessert spoonful. The Turkish "teaspoon"—çay kaşığı—is tiny, what Americans would use for a demi-tasse of espresso coffee.)

Is this tablet chewable?
Bu tablet çiğnenebilir mi?

Could you please give me something (for) ... ?
... (için) bir şey verir misiniz?

Dry skin
Kuru cilt

Against mosquitoes
Sivrisineklere karşı

Fungus / Athlete's foot
Mantar

Diarrhea
İshal

Nausea
Bulantı

Cramps
Kramp

Stomachache
Mide ağrısı

HEALTH MATTERS

Headache
Baş ağrısı

Sore throat
Boğaz ağrısı

I have a runny nose.
Burnum akıyor.

INTRODUCTIONS

Introductions; Professions; Personal and Family Matters

INTRODUCTIONS

Welcome!
Hoş geldiniz! (Said by the person who welcomes the guest.)
Hoş bulduk! (Said by the arriving guest.)
[This two-part formula is absolutely standard.]

I would like to introduce you to Ahmet Ersoy.
Sizi Ahmet Ersoy ile tanıştırmak istiyorum.

Ali Bey, I would like to introduce Gül Bayar to you.
Ali Bey, size Gül Bayar'ı tanıştırmak istiyorum.
(Note: The use of the first name followed by **Bey**, for a man, or **Hanım**, for a woman, has the same formality as English Mr., Ms., Mrs., or Miss + Surname. In contrast with English, the term "**Hanım**" does not indicate marital status.)

I am pleased to meet you. (How do you do?)
Memnun oldum. (*lit.* I have become pleased.)

I am pleased to have met you.
Tanıştığımıza memnun oldum. (*lit.* I have become pleased at our having met.)

What is your name?
İsminiz ne? / Adınız ne?

My name is Ayşe Kaya.
İsmim Ayşe Kaya. / Adım Ayşe Kaya.

Where are you from?
Nerelisiniz?

INTRODUCTIONS

I am from Istanbul.
İstanbulluyum.

I am from America; I am an American.
Amerikalıyım.

I am from Canada; I am a Canadian.
Kanadalıyım.

PROFESSIONS

Profession
Meslek

What is your profession?
Mesleğiniz ne?

What work do you do? (What is your work?)
Ne iş yapıyorsunuz?

I am a teacher.
Öğretmenim.

I am a violinist.
Kemancıyım.

I am a(n) ...
... (y)im. *(-im/-ım/-üm/-um)* [Insert "**y**" if the previous word ends with a vowel.]

Accountant
Muhasebeci

Artist
Sanatçı

Businessman
İşadamı

Doctor
Doktor

Engineer
Mühendis

PROFESSIONS

Farmer
Çiftçi

Housewife
Ev kadını / Ev hanımı

Journalist
Gazeteci

Lawyer
Avukat

Nurse
Hemşire

President of the Republic
Cumhurbaşkanı

Secretary
Sekreter

Soldier
Asker

Student
Öğrenci

PERSONAL AND FAMILY MATTERS

How is your family?
Aileniz nasıl?

Are you married?
Evli misiniz?

Yes, I am married.
Evet, evliyim.

No, I am not married; I am single.
Hayır, evli değilim; bekârım.

Do you have any children?
Çocuğunuz var mı?

No, I have no children.
Hayır, çocuğum yok.

Yes, I have three children: two girls and one boy.
Evet, üç çocuğum var: iki kız, bir oğlan.

I have two daughters and one son.
İki kızım, bir oğlum var.

FAMILY RELATIONSHIPS

Turkish has a more extensive vocabulary than English for indicating specific family relationships. Here are the most common:

Mother
Anne

FAMILY MATTERS

Father
Baba

Daughter
Kız

Son
Oğul

Spouse
Eş
(Frequently used; can mean either husband or wife.)

Wife
Karı

Husband
Koca

Paternal grandmother
Babaanne

Maternal grandmother
Anneanne

Grandfather
Büyükbaba / Dede
(Note: No distinction is made between paternal and maternal grandfathers.)

Paternal uncle (father's brother)
Amca

Maternal uncle (mother's brother)
Dayı

Paternal aunt (father's sister)
Hala

Maternal aunt (mother's sister)
Teyze

Uncle's wife; also sister-in-law (brother's wife)
Yenge

Aunt's husband; also brother-in-law (sister's husband)
Enişte

The husband of one's wife's sister
Bacanak

Nephew; niece
Yeğen

Male cousin
Kuzen

Female cousin
Kuzin

Language Matters

I did not understand.
Anlamadım.

I cannot understand.
Anlayamıyorum.

I do not know Turkish.
Türkçe bilmiyorum.

I know very little Turkish.
Çok az Türkçe biliyorum.

We speak a little Turkish.
Biraz Türkçe konuşuyoruz.

He doesn't know any Turkish at all.
Hiç Türkçe bilmez.

To learn Turkish is not easy.
Türkçe öğrenmek kolay değil.

It is a very difficult language.
Çok zor bir dil.

Do you know English?
İngilizce biliyor musunuz?

I prefer to speak French.
Fransızca konuşmayı tercih ederim.

Spanish (language)
İspanyolca

Arabic (language)
Arapça

Greek (language)
Yunanca

Russian (language)
Rusça

My French is better than my German.
Fransızcam Almancamdan daha iyi.

You are speaking too fast.
Çok hızlı konuşuyorsunuz.

Could you please speak a bit more slowly?
Biraz daha yavaş konuşabilir misiniz?

If you speak more slowly, I will probably understand.
(Eğer) daha yavaş konuşursanız, anlarım.

Would you say that again, please?
Tekrar söyler misiniz? / Tekrar eder misiniz?

What is this, in Turkish?
Türkçede bu ne demek? / Türkçede bu ne?

What is its name, in Turkish?
Türkçede bunun ismi ne?

TRANSPORTATION

Transportation (Air Travel; Taxis, Buses, Trains, the *Dolmuş*, and Ferries)

Bon voyage! Have a good trip!
İyi yolculuklar!

Travel agency
Seyahat acentası

Where can I buy tickets?
Nereden bilet alabilirim?

I would like to make a reservation.
Rezervasyon yaptırmak istiyorum.

AIR TRAVEL

Airport
Havalimanı / Havaalanı
(Both words are commonly used.)

I would like to go to the airport.
Havalimanına gitmek istiyorum.

Is the airport far from the city?
Havaalanı şehirden uzak mı?

Is there a bus that goes to the airport?
Havalimanına giden otobüs var mı?

Where does it leave from?
Nereden kalkıyor?

How often does the bus go to the airport?
Otobüs havalimanına ne kadar zamanda gider?

A bus leaves once every half hour.
Her yarım saatte bir, otobüs kalkıyor.

How long does it take to go to the airport?
Havaalanına gitmek ne kadar sürer?

Domestic terminal
İç hatlar terminali

International terminal
Dış hatlar terminali

Departing passengers
Giden yolcular

Arriving passengers
Gelen yolcular

Will the flight to Istanbul leave on time?
İstanbul uçağı zamanında hareket edecek mi?

The flight from Adana is twenty minutes late.
Adana'dan gelen uçak yirmi dakika gecikti.

The plane has not yet come.
Uçak daha gelmedi.

Passport control
Pasaport kontrolü

Customs
Gümrük

Is a visa required? Where can I get a visa?
Vize gerekir mi? Nereden vize alabilirim?

TRANSPORTATION

TAXIS

Taxis are plentiful. Prices, at least in the largest cities, are controlled by taxi meters. Rates are two: daytime (**gündüz**) from 6:00 A.M. until midnight; and night (**gece**), 50% higher, from midnight until 6:00 A.M. Certain cities permit taxis to and from the airport to charge the higher night rate, regardless of the time of day. Tips are not expected, but one can round up the figure. Dishonest taxi drivers are rare. However, one should be wary when hailing a taxi at, for example, the most popular tourist attractions in Istanbul (such as the Hagia Sophia) or at the central bus station in Ankara.

I would like a taxi please.
Bir taksi rica ediyorum.

(To) where are you going?
Nereye gidiyorsunuz?

I want to go to the bus station.
Otogara gitmek istiyorum.

Would you turn on the meter, please?
Taksimetreyi açar mısınız?

Why are you using the night rate? It is still daytime.
Niye gece ücreti kullanıyorsunuz? Hâlâ gündüz.

How much do I owe?
Borcum ne kadar?

I gave you five million liras.
Size beş milyon lira verdim.

Keep the change.
Üstü kalsın.

BUSES

Buses are the cheapest way to get around a city. In addition, the bus is the preferred mode of public transport between cities. The many private intercity bus companies offer frequent and convenient service. Smoking is forbidden. Seats are reserved. Most companies will seat single men and women with someone of the same sex. Long distance buses normally stop every two-three hours at a full-facility roadside restaurant for a rest stop. Food quality is typically good, prices reasonable.

Bus stop
Otobus durağı

Where is the nearest bus stop?
En yakın otobüs durağı nerede?

Which bus goes to Taksim?
Taksim'e hangi otobüs gider?

Where are bus tickets sold?
Otobüs biletleri nerede satılır?

Can I buy a ticket on the bus?
Otobüste bilet alabilir miyim?

How much is one ticket?
Bir bilet ne kadar?

I want to get off in Kızılay.
Kızılay'da inmek istiyorum.

Could you please tell me when I should get off?
Ne zaman inmem gerektiğini söyler misiniz?

TRANSPORTATION

Where is the bus station? (for intercity travel)
**Otogar nerede? / Garaj nerede? / Otobüs terminali
nerede?**

How much is a ticket for Konya?
Konya için bilet ne kadar?

Would you please give me two seats in the middle of
the bus?
Otobüsün ortalarından iki yer verir misiniz?

When does the bus for Trabzon leave?
Trabzon otobüsü saat kaçta hareket ediyor?

The bus will leave from platform no. 45.
Otobüs 45 nolu perondan kalkacak.

Where and when will the bus stop?
Otobüs nerede ve ne zaman duracak?

How much time do we have at this stop?
Bu durakta ne kadar zamanımız var?

This rest stop will be for forty minutes.
Bu mola kırk dakika olacak.

Where would you like to get off?
Nerede inmek istersiniz?

At the central bus station, or somewhere else?
Merkez terminalde mi, yoksa başka yerde mi?

If it is possible, I want to get off at the Bilkent bridge.
Mümkünse, Bilkent köprüsünde inmek istiyorum.

TRAINS

The railway system is much less developed than in western Europe. Nonetheless, certain lines, such as Istanbul-Ankara, have their devotees, for both the daytime journey and the overnight trip (for which compartments can be reserved). Prices are much less than the airplane, and in bad weather conditions the relative safety of trains is attractive.

The train station is a beautiful and historic building.
Gar güzel ve tarihi bir bina.

In which railway car is my seat?
Yerim hangi vagonda?

At which door should I get on, the front or the back?
Hangi kapıdan binmem lazım, ön mü, arka mı?

My suitcase is very heavy. Would you please help me carry it?
Valizim çok ağır. Taşımama yardım eder misiniz?

Is there a restaurant car?
Restoran vagonu var mı? / Yemekli vagon var mı?

Would you keep an eye on my things while I am in the restroom?
Ben tuvaletteyken eşyalarıma göz kulak olur musunuz?

Yes, sir, everything is fine.
Evet, efendim, her şey iyi. / Evet, efendim, her şey yolunda.

I am very comfortable, thank you.
Çok rahatım, teşekkür ederim.

TRANSPORTATION

THE *DOLMUŞ*

The **dolmuş** is a shared taxi or mini-van that plies a fixed route. The *dolmuş* leaves not on a fixed schedule, but when the driver decides that he has enough clients to make the trip worth his while. People can get on or off at almost any point. Prices are fixed by the municipality. Passengers pass their fare money up to the driver.

Do you go to Beşiktaş?
Beşiktaş'a gidiyor musunuz?

How much is it to Sıhhiye?
Sıhhiye'ye ne kadar?

I want to get off.
İnecek var. (*lit.* There is someone who will get off.)

I will get out at the stop.
Durakta ineceğim.

At a convenient place (... I would like to get off).
Müsait bir yerde.

FERRIES

Ferries have always been an important means of transportation in Istanbul and Izmir, in particular. They are still the only way to cross the Dardanelles.

Ferry
Vapur (*Passengers only; no cars*)

Car ferry
Feribot / Araba vapuru

High speed passenger ferry
Deniz otobüsü (*lit.* sea bus)

Dock
İskele

Because of fog, the ferryboats are not running today.
Sis nedeniyle, bugün vapur çalışmıyor.

When does the Üsküdar ferry leave?
Üsküdar vapuru ne zaman kalkıyor?

What are the departure times for the Üsküdar ferry?
Üsküdar vapurunun kalkış saatleri neler?

At what time is the first (last) ferry?
İlk (Son) vapur kaçta?

How long does it take to cross to Çanakkale?
Çanakkale'ye geçmek ne kadar sürer?

I would like two tickets.
İki bilet istiyorum.

Is there a student discount?
Öğrenci indirimi var mı?

I have a student card.
Öğrenci kartım var.

THE CAR

The Car

Do you have a car?
Arabanız var mı?

Yes, I have a car.
Evet, arabam var.

No, I don't have a car.
Hayır, arabam yok.

This new car is mine.
Bu yeni araba benim.

I would like to rent a car.
Araba kiralamak istiyorum.

Let the car be big, not small.
Araba büyük olsun, küçük değil.
(Note: This use of **olsun**, "let/may it be," is a common way of expressing a qualifying description.)

How much is the car rental fee per day?
Arabanın günlük kirası ne kadar?

How much is the car rental fee per week?
Arabanın haftalık kirası ne kadar?

Driver's license
Ehliyet / Sürücü belgesi

Could I please see your driver's license?
Ehliyetinizi (sürücü belgenizi) görebilir miyim?

International driver's license
Uluslararası ehliyet

Car registration booklet
Araba ruhsatı

Insurance; traffic insurance (= liability insurance)
Sigorta; trafik sigortası

Where is a parking lot (parking place)?
Park yeri nerede?

Can I leave the car here?
Arabayı burada bırakabilir miyim?

Where is the nearest gas station?
En yakın benzin istasyonu nerede?

Fill the tank, please.
Doldurun, lütfen.

Which would you like? Super, normal, or lead-free gasoline?
Hangisini (hangisinden) istersiniz? Süper, normal, veya kurşunsuz benzin?

Diesel fuel?
Motorin?

The car is not working.
Araba çalışmıyor.

We are looking for a repairman.
Tamirci arıyoruz.

Could you repair it?
(Onu) tamir edebilir misiniz?
(Note: Use **onu**, "it," if you are referring to some specific feature. If you mean repair in a general way, **onu** is not necessary.)

THE CAR

Could the problem be with the motor, I wonder? Or with the electric system?
Problem motorla ilgili olabilir mi, acaba? Veya elektrik sistemiyle?

Would you please check the car's oil?
Arabanın yağını kontrol eder misiniz?

Would you please check ... ?
... kontrol eder misiniz?

... the radiator.
Radyatörü ...

... the brakes.
Frenleri ...

... the headlights.
Farları ...

... the car battery.
Aküyü (= akümülatörü) ...

... the tires.
Lastikleri ...

The car has run out of gas.
Arabanın benzini bitti.

I have a flat tire.
Lastik patladı. (*lit.* A tire has exploded.)

We have had an accident.
Kaza geçirdik.

My car has been stolen. Where is the nearest police station?
Arabam çalındı. En yakın karakol nerede?

Car wash
Araba yıkama

This car needs to be washed.
Bu arabanın yıkanması lazım.

STAYING IN A HOTEL

Staying in a Hotel

I am looking for a good hotel.
İyi bir otel arıyorum.

Could you please recommend a good hotel in Antalya?
Antalya'da iyi bir otel tavsiye edebilir misiniz?

Room
Oda

A single room
Tek kişilik oda

Would you like a single room or a double room?
Tek kişilik oda mı yoksa çift kişilik oda mı istersiniz?

Do you have a double room?
Çift kişilik odanız var mı?

Instead of one big bed, we would like two separate beds.
Bir büyük yatak yerine iki ayrı yatak istiyoruz.

I would like a room with a sea view.
Deniz manzaralı bir oda istiyorum.

It will be more expensive.
Daha pahalı olur.

How much is a room per day?
Bir odanın bir günlük ücreti ne kadar?

We shall stay for three days.
Üç gün kalacağız.

Is there a discount for teachers?
Öğretmen indirimi var mı?

Do you accept credit cards?
Kredi kartı kabul ediyor musunuz?

Is there a laundry service?
Çamaşır yıkama servisi var mı?

Where is breakfast served?
Kahvaltı nerede verilir?

Would you please bring ... ?
... getirir misiniz?

Soap
Sabun

(Drinking) glass
Bardak

Clean sheets
Temiz çarşaf

Blanket
Battaniye

Lightbulb
Ampul

Would you please bring two towels to Room no. 158?
158 numaralı odaya iki havlu getirir misiniz?

The faucet is leaking.
Musluk akıtıyor.

The heating/air conditioner doesn't work.
Kalorifer/Klima çalışmıyor.

Could someone please come and look at it?
Birisi gelip, ona bakabilir mi?

Telephone, Post Office, and Internet Services

To telephone / To make a telephone call
Telefon etmek / Telefon açmak

My friend would like to make a telephone call.
Arkadaşım telefon etmek istiyor.

I want to call İzmir.
İzmir'e telefon etmek istiyorum.

Do you know the telephone number?
Telefon numarasını biliyor musunuz?

If I had a telephone directory, I would find it quickly.
Telefon rehberim olsaydı, onu çabuk bulurdum.

Is this a metered telephone or does it work with tokens?
Bu telefon kontörlü mü yoksa jetonlu mu?
(Note: Such telephones are found especially in post offices and small grocery shops.)

No, you must use a phone card.
Hayır, telefon kartı kullanmanız gerekiyor.

Where are telephone cards sold?
Telefon kartı nerede satılır?

I would like to speak with Erkan Çelik.
Erkan Çelik'le konuşmak istiyorum.

One moment, please.
Bir dakika, lütfen.

COMMUNICATIONS

He is not in his office right now. Would you like to leave a message?
Şu anda ofisinde değil. Mesaj bırakmak ister misiniz?

Would you please tell him to telephone Enver Türkmen?
Enver Türkmen'e telefon etmesini söyler misiniz?

He is not answering.
Cevap vermiyor.

A wrong number
Yanlış numara

I would like to send a FAX.
FAX çekmek istiyorum.

Where is the nearest post office?
En yakın postane (PTT) nerede?

Is it open on Saturdays?
Cumartesi günü açık mı?

I want to send these four letters to Canada.
Bu dört mektubu Kanada'ya göndermek istiyorum.

If I send the letters by express mail (**acele posta servisi**), when will they arrive in Canada?
Mektupları acele posta servisiyle gönderirsem, ne zaman Kanada'ya varır?

Postage stamp
Pul

Would you please give me five 500,000 lira stamps?
Bana beş tane beşyüzlük pul verir misiniz?

I am interested in postage stamps. I have a stamp collection.
Pullarla ilgileniyorum. Pul koleksiyonum var.

Could you please show me some interesting stamps?
Bana birkaç ilginç pul gösterebilir misiniz?

I would like this letter to be registered.
Bu mektubun taahhütlü olmasını istiyorum.

This package is too heavy. We cannot accept it.
Bu paket fazla ağır. Onu kabul edemiyoruz.

The central post office for packages
Merkez paket postanesi

It needs to be sent from the central package post office in Yenimahalle.
Yenimahalle'deki merkez paket postanesinden gönderilmesi gerekiyor.

I want to pick up my package.
Paketimi almak istiyorum.

Where can I find an Internet café?
İnternet Cafe nerede bulunur?
(*lit.* Where is an Internet café to be found?)

How does it work? I want to send e-mail (messages).
Nasıl çalışıyor? E-mail (mesajları) göndermek istiyorum.

The computer is turned on this way.
Bilgisayar böyle açılıyor.

When you have finished, turn off the computer.
Bitince, bilgisayarı kapatın.

COMMUNICATIONS

How much is the hourly fee for using the Internet?
İnternetin bir saatlik kullanım ücreti ne kadar?

Two and a half million Turkish liras per hour.
Bir saati ikibuçuk milyon Türk lirası.

In a Restaurant

TRADITIONAL TYPES OF RESTAURANTS

Snack bar
Büfe
Dishes offered may include: **tost** (grilled cheese or spicy **sucuk** sausage sandwiches); cold sandwiches; **döner** sandwiches (beef or chicken grilled on a vertical spit); **kumpir** (baked potatoes with cheese and Russian salad toppings); **dürüm** (like a flour tortilla wrap); **gözleme** (pancake wrap, often fried); freshly squeezed orange juice; **ayran** (a slightly salted yogurt drink); other non-alcoholic drinks; and tea and Nescafé.

Pastry shop
Pastane
Pastry shops will serve traditional desserts such as **baklava**, layers of phyllo filled with pistachios (**fıstıklı**) or with walnuts (**cevizli**); **tel kedayif** (a sort of sugary Shredded Wheat); **sütlaç** (rice pudding); **aşure** (an unusual pudding with dried fruit, beans, and nuts, no milk); and, in the month of Ramazan only, **güllaç** (a rose-flavored milk pudding). Western-style cakes (**pasta**) and cookies (**kurabiye**, both sweet, **tatlı**, and savory, **tuzlu**) and miscellaneous savory buns (such as **poğaça**, a breakfast favorite) are also standard. Tea, coffee, and other non-alcoholic drinks are sold.

Simple restaurant specializing in grilled meat.
Kebap salonu
Dishes offered typically include: lentil soup; **şiş kebab** (chunks of beef, lamb, or chicken on a skewer, grilled); **şiş köfte** (ground beef or lamb, on a skewer, grilled); possibly **İskender kebap** (**döner kebap** with

tomato sauce and butter, accompanied by bulgur and yogurt); salad; and one dessert (such as **tel kedayif**, see above). Beverages include water, **ayran**, and soft drinks. Tea usually available. No alcoholic drinks. Prices are very reasonable, service rapid.

Simple restaurant specializing in flat pizza-like bread (**pide**) with various toppings.

Pide salonu

Dishes offered typically include **pide** with either yellow cheese, ground beef, or small beef chunks, plus the menu of the kebap salonu given above. Reasonable prices, and quick service.

More formal restaurants, with a full range of appetizers and main courses.

Lokanta / Restoran

For a leisurely lunch or dinner. Prices range from moderate on up. Small dishes of cold appetizers (**meze**) are brought on a tray (**tepsi**). Diners at a table choose what they would like. Salads and hot appetizers are ordered separately. These appetizers are shared by all. The main course is not ordered at the beginning, but only later, when the appetizers have been largely finished. Main dishes can be ordered as individual portions (such as **şiş kebab**, **şiş köfte**, or other types of grilled fish, chicken, and meat) or as a group dish (such as a meat and vegetable stew, **güveç**; braised meat, **kavurma**; or a fish stew, **buğulama**). Dessert, ordered when the main course is finishing, is typically fresh fruit (**meyve**). Alcoholic beverages are normally available: **rakı** (an anise-flavored drink, mixed with water), beer, and wine. Note that **rakı** is drunk throughout the meal; in contrast with European custom, **rakı** is not a pre-dinner cocktail to be followed by wine.

IN A RESTAURANT

Could you recommend a good restaurant?
İyi bir lokanta tavsiye edebilir misiniz?

Is the restaurant open?
Lokanta açık mı?

Is there a (free) place?
(Boş) yer var mı?

We would like to sit by the window.
Pencerenin yanında oturmak istiyoruz.

Could we sit outside?
Dışarıda oturabilir miyiz?

Is that table free?
Şu masa boş mu?

We are four people.
Dört kişiyiz.

We are six people, including two children.
Altı kişiyiz, iki de çocuk var. / İki çocukla beraber, altı kişiyiz.

Where is the bathroom? Where is the washroom (sink)?
Tuvalet nerede? Lavabo nerede?

Breakfast
Kahvaltı

Lunch
Öğle yemeği (*lit.* midday meal)

Dinner
Akşam yemeği (*lit.* evening meal)

IN A RESTAURANT

Menu
Yemek listesi

Could we look at the menu, please?
Yemek listesine bakabilir miyiz?

Would you please bring ... ?
... getirir misiniz?

Napkins
Peçete

Bread
Ekmek

Salt and pepper
Tuz ve biber

This glass is dirty. Please bring a clean glass.
Bu bardak kirli. Temiz bir bardak getirin, lütfen.

Knife
Bıçak

Fork
Çatal

Spoon
Kaşık

Plate
Tabak

Excuse me!
Bakar mısınız? (*lit*. Would you look?)
(<u>Note</u>: The standard phrase used to get the attention of a
waiter, or indeed of a salesperson in any store.)

Have you ordered?
a) **Sipariş verdiniz mi?**
b) **Söylediniz mi?**

Yes, we have ordered.
a) **Evet, verdik.**
b) **Evet, söyledik.**

No, we have not yet ordered.
a) **Hayır, henüz vermedik.**
b) **Hayır, henüz söylemedik.**

Alright, we are ready. We have decided.
Tamam, hazırız. Karar verdik.

What would you like?
Ne arzu edersiniz?

For breakfast we give tea or coffee, fresh bread, cheese, tomatoes, olives, butter, jam, and honey.
Kahvaltı için çay veya kahve, taze ekmek, peynir, domates, zeytin, tereyağı, reçel, ve bal veriyoruz.

I will have ...
... alacağım.

Soup
Çorba

Lentil soup
Mercimek çorbası

Tomato soup
Domates çorbası

Green salad
Yeşil salata

Salad of lettuce, shredded carrots, and red cabbage
Mevsim salatası

Shepherd salad (chopped tomatoes and cucumbers)
Çoban salatası

What meze do you have?
Meze olarak ne var? (*lit.* As meze, what is there?)
(Note: **Meze** are appetizers, both cold and hot; restaurants will often have a tray loaded with sample dishes; you pick which you would like and share them with your fellow diners.)

Would you bring the meze tray, please?
Meze tepsisini getirir misiniz?

Let's take eggplant salad, white (feta) cheese, and marinated dried beans.
Patlıcan salatası, beyaz peynir, ve pilaki alalım.

Do you have lamb shish kebab?
Kuzu şiş (kebap) var mı?
(Note: Here the word "**kebap**" is understood, so no need to say it.)

I'd like the meat well done.
Et iyi pişmiş olsun. (*lit.* Let the meat be well cooked.)

I would prefer chicken shish kebab.
Piliç şiş tercih ederim.

Would you please bring a large portion of spicy Adana kebap?
Bir buçuk acılı Adana kebap getirir misiniz?
(Note: **Bir buçuk**, *lit.* "one and a half," is said when ordering a large portion of kebab, instead of the normal

"one"—**bir**—portion. **Adana kebap**, the specialty of the city of Adana, is ground lamb grilled on a skewer; it can be ordered spicy, **acılı**, or non-spicy, **acısız**.)

Is the pide with ground meat and chopped tomato topping good?
Kıymalı pide güzel mi?
(Note: **Pide** is flat bread, served plain or with toppings, commonly ground meat (**kıymalı pide**), small meat chunks (**kuşbaşılı pide**), or yellow cheese (**kaşarlı pide**). A close and popular relative of **kıymalı pide** is called **lahmacun**.)

My spouse (= wife/husband) would like grilled bonito (sea bass).
Eşim palamut (levrek) ızgara istiyor.

My friend does not like French-fried potatoes.
Arkadaşım patates tava sevmez.

My daughter is a vegetarian. What meatless dishes do you have?
Kızım vejetaryen. Etsiz yemek olarak ne var?
(Note: The vegetarian traveling in Turkey should keep in mind that **et**, "meat," refers especially to red meat rather than to chicken (**piliç** or **tavuk**), or fish (**balık**).)

My brother wants a salad without onions.
Kardeşim soğansız salata istiyor.

Would you like a (cooked) dessert or fresh fruit?
Tatlı veya meyve ister misiniz?

I shall take the fresh fruit plate.
Meyve tabağı alayım.

What would you like to drink?
Ne içersiniz?

IN A RESTAURANT

Water
Su

Mineral water (soda water)
Maden suyu

Coca cola (and related drinks)
Kola

Ice cold
Buz gibi

With ice
Buzlu

Without ice
Buzsuz

Fruit juice
Meyve suyu

Orange juice
Portakal suyu

Cherry juice
Vişne suyu

Apple juice
Elma suyu

Apricot juice
Kayısı suyu

Peach juice
Şeftali suyu

Beer
Bira

Raki (an anise-flavored alcoholic drink)
Rakı

A "double" of rakı (= the normal serving).
Bir duble rakı.

One bottle of red wine.
Bir şişe kırmızı şarap.

A small bottle of white wine, please.
Küçük şişe beyaz şarap, lütfen.

Tea
Çay

Coffee
Kahve

Turkish coffee: plain (no sugar), medium (some sugar), sweet (generous with the sugar)
Türk kahvesi: sade, orta, şekerli

Nescafé with milk.
Sütlü Nescafe.

No sugar, please.
Şekersiz olsun. (*lit.* Let it be without sugar.)

The bill, please.
Hesap, lütfen.

Would you bring the bill, please?
Hesabı getirir misiniz?

IN A RESTAURANT

Is service included?
Servis dahil mi?

Is a 10% tip appropriate?
Yüzde on bahşiş uygun mu?
(Answer: In restaurants and hairdressers/barbers, yes. In taxis, however, no tip is expected; round up, if desired.)

The food was delicious. My compliments!
Yemek çok nefisti. Elinize sağlık!

To eat dinner in a good restaurant is truly wonderful.
İyi bir lokantada akşam yemeği yemek gerçekten harika.

Shopping

Could I help you?
Size yardım edebilir miyim?

I am looking for a bookstore.
Kitabevi arıyorum.

I am looking for a ...
... arıyorum.

Clothing store
Giyim mağazası

Florist
Çiçekçi

Jewelry store
Kuyumcu

Market; market place; bazaar
Pazar

Shoe repair shop
Ayakkabı tamircisi / Kunduracı

Stationery and office supplies store
Kırtasiye

Tailor
Terzi

Traditional handicrafts shop
Geleneksel el sanatları dükkânı

SHOPPING

IN A BOOKSTORE

I am looking for a map of Istanbul.
İstanbul haritası arıyorum.

Do you sell a map of Turkey?
Türkiye haritası satıyor musunuz?

I would like to buy a guidebook to Ephesus.
Efes rehberi almak istiyorum.

Do you have a Turkish-English dictionary?
Türkçe-İngilizce sözlüğü var mı?

Do you have English language books?
İngilizce kitaplarınız var mı?

Do you sell English language books?
İngilizce kitap satıyor musunuz?

IN A STATIONERY STORE

I would like to buy a notebook.
Defter almak istiyorum.

Envelopes
Zarf

Pen
Kalem

Pencil
Kurşunkalem

Eraser
Silgi

IN A CLOTHING STORE

I want/would like to buy ...
... almak istiyorum.

I want/would like to buy a shirt.
Gömlek almak istiyorum.

Belt
Kemer

Dress
Elbise

Jacket
Ceket

Pants
Pantalon

Shoes
Ayakkabı

Socks
Çorap

Stockings (panty hose)
Külotlu çorap

Suit (lady's)
Takım / Tayyör

Suit (man's)
Takım elbise

Sweater
Kazak

Swimsuit
Mayo

Underwear
İç çamaşırı

I wear size 42.
42 (kırkiki) beden giyiyorum.

I don't know Turkish sizes.
Türkiye'deki bedenleri bilmiyorum.

Could you please measure me?
Ölçülerimi alır mısınız? (*lit.* Would you please take my measurements?)

Could I try it on?
Prova edebilir miyim?

These pants are rather loose.
Bu pantalon oldukça bol.

This size did not fit me. Do you have a smaller (bigger) size?
Bu boy bana uymadı. Daha küçük (daha büyük) bir boy var mı?

PRICES AND PAYMENT

How much?
Kaça? / Kaç lira? / Ne kadar?

It is very expensive.
Çok pahalı.

Do you have something cheaper?
Daha ucuz bir şey var mı?

If there is a cheaper shirt, I will buy it.
(Eğer) daha ucuz bir gömlek varsa, onu alacağım.

Even if there is a cheaper dress, she will not buy it.
Daha ucuz bir elbise olsa da, onu almayacak.

If there had been a cheaper pair of pants, I would have bought them.
(Eğer) daha ucuz bir pantalon olsaydı, onu alırdım.

How much is the total?
Toplam ne kadar?

Do you have change?
Bozuk paranız var mı?

Unfortunately, I don't (have any).
Maalesef, yok.

I gave you ten million liras, but you gave (me) only two million.
Size on milyon lira verdim, fakat yalnız ikimilyon verdiniz.

I am waiting for the bill.
Hesabı bekliyorum.

We are waiting for our change.
Bozuk paramızı bekliyoruz.

Would you please give (me) a receipt?
Fiş verir misiniz?

SHOPPING

I would like to request an invoice (formal receipt).
Fatura rica ediyorum.

Cash money
Nakit

Credit card
Kredi kartı

Full advance payment / Down payment
Peşin

(Paying) in installments
Taksitle

VAT included.
KDV dahil.
(Note: The **KDV—katma değer vergisi—**is the value-added tax [VAT], better known to Americans as the sales tax.)

Markets: Buying Food

DIFFERENT TYPES OF FOOD SHOPS

Fruit and vegetable market
Manav

Small grocery shop
Bakkal

Butcher's
Kasap

Grocery store (could be either small or large)
Market

Pastry shop; bakery (for cakes, cookies, specialty savory breads and biscuits, but not regular loaf bread)
Pastane

Bakery (for bread)
Fırın

USEFUL PHRASES

Would you please give (me) one kilo of ripe tomatoes?
Bir kilo olgun domates verir misiniz?

How many oranges would you like?
Kaç tane portakal istersiniz?

I will take four.
Dört tane alacağım.
(Note: The word "**tane**" variously means "seed," "grain," "item," or "unit," and is commonly used with numbers or

with the question word **kaç,** "how many," as in the examples here.)

These peaches are as hard as rocks. I'm not buying them.
Bu şeftaliler taş gibi sert. Onları almıyorum.

Do you sell whole wheat bread?
Kepek ekmeği satıyor musunuz?

Unfortunately, we have none left.
Maalesef, kalmadı. (*lit.* Unfortunately, it didn't remain.)

Is the fish fresh?
Balık taze mi?

I would like a half kilo of lean ground beef.
Yarım kilo yağsız dana kıyma istiyorum.

Would you recommend the lamb chops?
Kuzu pirzola tavsiye eder misiniz?

Would you please cut the chicken into pieces?
Pilici (Tavuğu) parçalar mısınız? / Pilici (Tavuğu) parçalara ayırır mısınız?

FOOD ITEMS TO BUY MIGHT INCLUDE:

Fruit	**Meyve**
Apples	**Elma**
Apricots	**Kayısı**
Bananas	**Muz**
Cherries	**Kiraz**

(Sweet, for eating; as opposed to **vişne,** the sour cherries used for juice and jam.)

Figs	İncir
Grapes	Üzüm
Peaches	Şeftali
Strawberries	Çilek
Watermelon	Karpuz
Yellow melon	Kavun
Vegetables	Sebze
Cabbage	Lahana
Carrots	Havuç
Cauliflower	Karnabahar
Chickpeas; garbanzos	Nohut
Curly lettuce	Kıvırcık salata
Dried beans	Kuru fasulye
Eggplant	Patlıcan
Garlic	Sarmısak
Green beans	Taze fasulye (*lit.* fresh beans)
Green peppers	Yeşil biber
Leeks	Pırasa
Onions	Soğan
Parsley	Maydanoz
Potatoes	Patates
Romaine lettuce	Marul
Spinach	Ispanak
Tomatoes	Domates
Zucchini squash	Kabak
Bread	Ekmek
Butter	Tereyağı
Cheese	Peynir
Corn meal	Mısır unu
Egg(s)	Yumurta
Flour	Un
Hazelnut spread; hazelnut butter	Fındık ezmesi

Honey	**Bal**
Jam	**Reçel**
Milk	**Süt**
Skim milk	**Yağsız süt**
Mustard	**Hardal**
Olive(s)	**Zeytin**
Olive oil	**Zeytin yağı**
Pasta	**Makarna**

(<u>Note</u>: The Turkish word **pasta** = "cake.")

Pepper	**Biber**
Rice (uncooked)	**Pirinç**

(<u>Note</u>: Cooked rice = **pilav**.)

Salt	**Tuz**
Sugar	**Şeker**
Sunflower oil	**Ayçiçeği yağı**
Tomato paste	**Domates salçası**
Vinegar	**Sirke**
Yogurt	**Yoğurt**

Meat	**Et**
Fish	**Balık**
Chicken	**Piliç / Tavuk**
Turkey	**Hindi**
Beef	**Dana**
Lamb	**Kuzu**
Pork	**Domuz eti**
Ground meat	**Kıyma**
Meat in small chunks	**Kuşbaşı**
Fatty meat	**Yağlı et**
Lean meat	**Yağsız et**
Chops	**Pirzola**
Steak	**Biftek / Bonfile**
Breast	**Göğüs**
Filet	**Fileto**

MARKETS: BUYING FOOD

OTHER PRODUCTS SOLD IN GROCERIES INCLUDE:

Cigarettes
Sigara

Bleach
Çamaşır suyu

Detergent
Deterjan

Dishwashing soap
Bulaşık deterjanı

Kleenex
Kağıt mendil / Selpak (a brand name)

Lightbulbs
Ampul

Matches
Kibrit

Newspaper
Gazete

Telephone card
Telefon kartı

Toilet paper
Tuvalet kağıdı

Sight-seeing

Where is the Tourist Information Office?
Turizm Danışma Ofisi nerede?

We would like to hire an English-speaking guide.
İngilizce bilen bir rehber tutmak istiyoruz.

I would like to buy a good map of the city.
Şehrin iyi bir haritasını almak istiyorum.

To tour (a place), walk around (a place)
Gezmek

Excursion, outing, tour
Gezi

Historical places / Monuments
Tarihi yerler / Anıtlar

I have only one day in Konya. Which historical places
would you recommend that I tour?
**Konya'da yalnız bir günüm var. Hangi tarihi yerleri
gezmemi tavsiye edersiniz?**

From when to when are the ruins of Ephesus open?
·Efes harabeleri saat kaçtan kaça açık?

I am interested in …
… ile ilgileniyorum.

Museums
Müzeler

Ruins
Harabeler

Hittite archaeology
Hitit arkeolojisi

The history of the Roman Empire
Roma İmparatorluğunun tarihi

Byzantine, Seljuk, and Ottoman architecture
Bizans, Selçuk, ve Osmanlı mimarlığı

Mosques
Camiler

Churches
Kiliseler

Art
Sanat

Sculpture
Heykel / Heykeltıraşlık

Natural monuments; natural wonders
Doğal anıtlar

What is its date?
Bunun tarihi ne?

Fifteenth century B.C.
15. yy. M.Ö. (onbeşinci yüzyıl milattan önce)

A.D.
M.S. (milattan sonra)

Camping and Hiking

Where is a campground?
Kamp yeri nerede?

Can we camp here?
Burada kamp yapabilir miyiz?

Camping is forbidden.
Kamp yapmak yasaktır.

Can I set up my tent here?
Çadırımı buraya kurabilir miyim?

When will the noise end?
Gürültü ne zaman biter?

Do you have a quiet (*lit.* noiseless) place?
Gürültüsüz bir yeriniz var mı?

How much are the campground fees?
Kamping ücretleri ne kadar?

What services are included?
Hangi hizmetler dahil?

Where is an electric outlet?
Elektrik prizi nerede?

Where are the showers? Where are the toilets?
Duş nerede? Tuvalet nerede?

Is there a grocery store here?
Burada bakkal var mı?

Is there minibus service from this campground?
Bu kamp yerinden minibüs servisi var mı?

Do you have a laundry service?
Çamaşır servisiniz var mı?

Where shall I throw out the garbage?
Çöpü nereye atayım?

Is the water safe to drink?
Su içilebilir mi?

Can one fish here?
Burada balık avlanır mı?

Do we need to take precautions against wild animals, snakes, or scorpions?
Vahşi hayvanlar, yılanlar, veya akreplere karşı tedbir almamız gerekiyor mu?

Are the hiking trails clearly marked?
Yürüyüş patikaları belli mi?

Road, way
Yol

Would you please show me the way?
Yolu gösterir misiniz?

Which road goes to the village?
Hangi yol köye gidiyor?

It is very dangerous to climb that mountain without a guide.
Şu dağı rehber olmadan tırmanmak çok tehlikeli.

CAMPING AND HIKING

A storm is expected. Be careful!
Fırtına bekleniyor. Dikkat edin!

The sunset is magnificent!
Güneşin batışı muhteşem!

Money and Banking

Money
Para

Turkish lira (<u>Note</u>: The <u>lira</u> is the unit of currency.)
Türk lirası

Bank
Banka

Where is the nearest bank?
En yakın banka nerede?

Where can I find a foreign currency office?
Nerede döviz bürosu bulabilirim?

Where is the currency exchange?
Kambiyo nerede?

I want to change dollars.
Dolar bozdurmak istiyorum.

Would you please give (me) Turkish liras?
Türk lirası verir misiniz?

Currency exchange rate
Kur

What is today's exchange rate?
Bugünkü kur ne?

How many Turkish liras per dollar?
Bir dolar'ın Türk lirası karşılığı ne kadar?

MONEY AND BANKING

Dollar
Dolar

Euro
Euro

English pounds (sterling)
İngiliz sterlini

German marks
Alman markı

I want to deposit thirty million lira into my account.
Hesabıma otuz milyon lira yatırmak istiyorum.

I want to withdraw 500 million Turkish liras from my account.
Hesabımdan beşyüzmilyon Türk lirası çekmek istiyorum.

Do you have change?
Bozuk paranız var mı?

I am afraid of receiving counterfeit money.
Sahte para almaktan korkuyorum.

Would you please change this ten million banknote?
Bu onmilyonluk bankınotu bozar mısınız?

Cash
Nakit

Money transfer; money order
Havale

MONEY AND BANKING

I want to send a money order to Canada.
Kanada'ya havale göndermek istiyorum.

Would you please fill out this form?
Bu formu doldurur musunuz?

Signature
İmza

Would you please sign here? And on the back?
Burayı imzalar mısınız? Ve arkayı?

Where is the closest ATM?
En yakın ATM nerede?

HAIRDRESSER/BARBER/BATH

Hairdresser, Barber, and Public Bath; Toiletries

Hairdresser's
Kuaför

Barbershop
Erkek kuaförü / Berber salonu

Public bath; traditional Turkish bath
Hamam

AT THE HAIRDRESSER'S AND BARBER'S

I would like to have my hair cut.
Saçımı kestirmek istiyorum.

But not too short.
Ama fazla kısa olmasın.

Would you please wash my hair? / I would like my hair washed.
Saçımı yıkar mısınız? / Saçımı yıkatmak istiyorum.

I would like to get a shave.
Tıraş olmak istiyorum.

I would like a manicure.
Manikür yaptırmak istiyorum.

Would you dye my hair blond (*lit.* yellow)?
Saçımı sarıya boyar mısınız?

At least once in my life I would like to treat my hair with henna.
Hayatımda en azından bir defa saçıma kına yakmak istiyorum.

AT THE *HAMAM* (traditional Turkish bath)

Note: The traditional **hamam** is strictly segregated by sex, men only and women only. A large bath may have a separate section for each; smaller baths will have separate hours for men and women. In a distinct modification of tradition, unisex baths can be found in some touristic towns.

Cloth worn wrapped around the waist while one is in a **hamam**
Peştemal

Bath clogs/slippers, worn in a **hamam** (to avoid slipping on wet marble floors)
Nalın

Towel
Havlu

I would like to be washed (with the **kese**, a bath glove of rough cloth) and given a massage.
Kese ve masaj istiyorum.

I will wash myself. Do you have soap?
Kendim yıkanacağım. Sabun var mı?

TOILETRIES

TOILETRIES

Body lotion	**Vücut losyonu**
Comb	**Tarak**
Cream	**Krem**
For dry/normal/oily skin.	**Kuru/Normal/Yağlı cilt için.**
Deodorant	**Deodorant**
Depilatory wax	**Ağda**
Diapers	**Bebek bezi**
Hairbrush	**Saç fırçası**
Lipstick	**Ruj**
Make-up	**Makyaj**
Mirror	**Ayna**
Nail file	**Tırnak törpüsü**
Razor blade	**Tıraş bıçağı**
Safety razor; shaver	**Tıraş makinası**
Sanitary napkins	**Kadın bağı**
Shampoo	**Şampuan**
Shaving cream	**Tıraş kremi**
Soap	**Sabun**
Sponge	**Sünger**
Suntan lotion	**Güneş kremi**
Talcum powder	**Talk pudrası**
Tampons	**Tampon**
Tissues	**Kağıt mendil**
Toilet paper	**Tuvalet kağıdı**
Toothbrush	**Diş fırçası**
Toothpaste	**Diş macunu**
Towel	**Havlu**
Tweezers	**Cımbız**

Sports and Entertainment

Which sports do you like?
Hangi sporları seviyorsunuz?

I love football very much.
Futbolu çok seviyorum.

My brother is a Galatasaray fan, but I am a Fenerbahçe fan.
Kardeşim Galatasaraylı, fakat ben Fenerbahçeliyim.

Turkish athletes have been very successful in weight-lifting and wrestling.
Türk sporcuları halterde ve güreşte çok başarılı.

Would you like to play tennis?
Tenis oynamak ister misiniz?

Do you play tennis?
Tenis oynuyor musunuz?

No, I don't play tennis.
Hayır, tenis oynamıyorum.

Let's play bridge!
Briç oynayalım!

Chess
Satranç

Backgammon
Tavla

Checkers
Dama

Pişti (a popular card game)
Pişti

Now I am tired. Is another time possible?
Şimdi yorgunum. Başka bir zaman mümkün mü?

Let's go swimming.
Yüzmeye gidelim.

Where is the swimming pool?
Havuz nerede?

There is no swimming pool here.
Burada havuz yok.

We shall swim in the lake.
Gölde yüzeceğiz.

The beach is beautiful.
Plaj çok güzel.

Is there a sandy beach?
Kumlu plaj var mı?

If we go to Bodrum, we can learn scuba diving.
Bodrum'a gidersek, dalmayı öğrenebiliriz.

Are you an experienced scuba diver?
Tecrübeli dalgıç mısınız?

Are lessons and equipment expensive?
Dersler ve ekipman pahalı mı?

Ask in the diving center at the beach.
Plajdaki dalgıçlık merkezine sorun.

In the winter I like to ski.
Kışın kayak yapmayı seviyorum.

My brother likes to ice skate.
Kardeşim buz pateni yapmayı seviyor.

Day trip
Günübirlik seyahat

Day trips to ski centers are possible both from Istanbul and from Ankara.
Hem İstanbul'dan hem Ankara'dan kayak merkezlerine günübirlik seyahatlar mümkün.

I need to rent skiing equipment.
Kayak takımı kiralamam lazım.

Skis, ski boots, and ski poles.
Kayak, kayak ayakkabısı, ve kayak sopası.

Can I take skiing lessons?
Kayak dersleri alabilir miyim?

What do you do in the evening in order to have fun?
Akşam eğlenmek için ne yapıyorsunuz?

I go to the movies.
Sinemaya giderim.

Where is the movie theater?
Sinema nerede?

Are there any seats for tonight?
Bu akşam için yer var mı?

My spouse (wife/husband) prefers opera and ballet.
Eşim opera ve bale tercih eder.

SPORTS/ENTERTAINMENT

My father likes to watch belly dancing.
Babam göbek dansı seyretmeyi seviyor.

Would you like to go dancing?
Dansa gitmek ister misiniz?

My son is going to the discotheque with his friends.
Oğlum arkadaşlarıyla diskoya gidiyor.

He will come home very late, won't he?
Eve çok geç gelecek, değil mi?

Yes, but he has a key. In addition, we told him to be quiet.
Evet, ama anahtarı var. Ayrıca, ona sessiz olmasını söyledik.

TIME/TIME EXPRESSIONS

Telling Time; Time Expressions

Second
Saniye

Minute
Dakika

Just a minute.
Bir dakika. (*if pronounced quickly*: bi dakka)
(Note: Used when a short wait is anticipated.)

Quarter hour
Çeyrek

Hour
Saat (Note: **Saat** also can mean "clock" or "watch.")

Morning
Sabah

Noon
Öğle

Afternoon
Öğleden sonra

Evening
Akşam

Night
Gece

What time is it?
Saat kaç?

TIME/TIME EXPRESSIONS

It is nine o'clock.
Saat dokuz.

It is 9:10.
Saat dokuzu on geçiyor. (*lit.* Ten is passing nine o'clock.)

It is twenty to nine (= 8:40).
Saat dokuza yirmi var. (*lit.* To nine o'clock there is twenty.)

The bus leaves at 5:30 in the afternoon.
Otobüs öğleden sonra beş buçukta hareket ediyor.

The train will arrive at 10:20 in the morning.
Tren sabah onu yirmi geçe gelecek.

The lecture started at 6:45 P.M.
Konferans yediye çeyrek kala başladı.

As soon as Ali Bey comes, we shall start.
Ali Bey gelir gelmez başlayacağız.

Whenever Ali Bey comes, we shall start then.
Ali Bey ne zaman gelirse, o zaman başlayacağız.

Day
Gün

Happy birthday!
Doğum gününüz kutlu olsun!

Age
Yaş

How old are you?
Kaç yaşındasınız?

I am twenty-nine years old.
Yirmidokuz yaşındayım.

Month
Ay (<u>Note</u>: This word can also mean "moon.")

January, February, March, April.
Ocak, Şubat, Mart, Nisan.

May, June, July, August.
Mayıs, Haziran, Temmuz, Ağustos.

September, October, November, December.
Eylül, Ekim, Kasım, Aralık.

Year
Yıl / Sene

Century
Yüzyıl

B.C.
M.Ö. (= milattan önce)

A.D.
M.S. (= milattan sonra)

Religious festival; holiday
Bayram

Have a happy holiday!
Bayramınız kutlu olsun!

Happy New Year!
Yeni yılınız kutlu olsun! / İyi seneler!

Vacation
Tatil

Have a good vacation!
İyi tatiller!

Weather

Weather; air
Hava

The weather is sunny.
Hava güneşli.

The weather is ...
Hava ...

cold
soğuk

hot
sıcak

rainy
yağmurlu

cloudy
bulutlu

foggy
sisli

snowy
karlı

humid
nemli

dry
kuru

WEATHER

Yesterday the weather was very cold. It was snowing.
Dün hava çok soğuktu. Kar yağıyordu.

If it had not rained, we would have eaten lunch outdoors.
Yağmur yağmasaydı, öğle yemeğini dışarıda yerdik.

Tomorrow the weather will be beautiful.
Yarın hava güzel olacak.